To Believe is to Pray

TO BELIEVE IS TO PRAY

Readings from Michael Ramsey

James E. Griffiss, editor

COWLEY PUBLICATIONS
Cambridge ✦ Boston
Massachusetts

Published in the United States of America by Cowley Publications, a division of the Society of St. John the Evangelist. No portion of this book may be reproduced, stored in or introduced into a retrieval system, or transmitted, in any form or by any means—including photocopying—without the prior written permission of Cowley Publications, except in the case of brief quotations embodied in critical articles and reviews.

Library of Congress Cataloging-in-Publication Data:
Ramsey, Michael, 1904-1988.
   To believe is to pray: readings / from Michael Ramsey; James E. Griffiss, editor.
      p.   cm.
   ISBN 1-56101-128-2
   1. Theology. 2. Anglican Communion—Doctrines. I. Griffiss, James E., 1928– .
   II. Title.
   BT80.R344   1996
   230'.3—dc20   96-35831

Sources:
Be Still and Know (London: Collins/Faith, 1982; Cambridge, Mass.: Cowley, 1993). *Canterbury Essays and Addresses* (London: SPCK, 1964). *Canterbury Pilgrim* (London: SPCK, 1974). *The Christian Priest Today* (London: SPCK, 1972; rev. ed. Cambridge, Mass: Cowley, 1987). *Come Holy Spirit,* with Cardinal Suenens (More-house-Barlow, 1976). *Durham Essays and Addresses* (London: SPCK, 1951). *An Era in Anglican Theology* (England, *From Gore to Temple)* (Scribners, 1960). *Freedom, Faith, and the Future* (London: SPCK, 1970). *The Future of the Christian Church.* with Cardinal Suenens (Wilton, Conn.: Morehouse-Barlow, 1970). *The Glory of God and the Transfiguration of Christ* (London: Longmans and Green, 1949). *God, Christ, and the World* (London: SCM, 1969). *The Gospel and the Catholic Church* (Cambridge, Mass.: Cowley, 1936/1990). *Holy Spirit* (Eerdmans, 1977, Cambridge, Mass.: Cowley, 1992). *Introducing the Christian Faith* (London: SCM, 1961). *The Resurrection of Christ* (Westminster, 1946). *Sacred and Secular* (New York: Harper and Row, 1965).

Editors: Cynthia Shattuck and Vicki Black; Designer: Vicki Black

This book is printed on recycled, acid-free paper and was produced in Canada.

Cowley Publications
28 Temple Place
Boston, Massachusetts 02111
1-800-225-1534

In Thanksgiving

Michael Ramsey
Joan Ramsey

A note from the editor

In the excerpts from Michael Ramsey's writings I have taken two liberties. First, in order that the selections may be read easily, I have avoided ellipses, except where the omissions are of considerable length. The references for each selection will enable readers to track down the omitted portions should they wish to do so. I do not believe I have omitted anything which is crucial or central to his thinking.

Second, I have, wherever possible or necessary, changed the text to make it more inclusive; thus, "he" and "man" have been changed except where the context or meaning requires them. While Bishop Ramsey wrote in the style of his own time, he was also, as I know from conversations with him, quite sensitive to the changes which the demands of a new time might require. Indeed, on many occasions in the following writings, he himself was careful to speak of men and women long before such usage became more customary. And, as we can know from all that he has written, he certainly would want the words he used in order to proclaim the Gospel to speak it clearly, rather than get in the way.

CONTENTS

INTRODUCTION

Over the centuries, Archbishops of Canterbury have been many things. As chief primates of the Church of England, their influence and power has largely been confined to Britain. And, with only a few exceptions, they have not been noted for eccentricity or for having strong and memorable personalities. Only a few—Anselm, Thomas Cranmer, William Laud, and William Temple come to mind—have contributed significantly to the theological work of the church. Most of them have been adept at ecclesiastical politics, guiding the Church of England through troubled times or presiding serenely over coronations and royal weddings and fulfilling other functions of the established church.

Michael Ramsey, the one hundredth Archbishop of Canterbury (from 1961 to his retirement in 1974) was one of the few exceptions. He was, first of all, a charismatic figure: he looked and acted like an archbishop, or, at least, the way western Anglicans think archbishops ought to look and act—slightly disheveled, portly, a ring of white hair around a bald pate, bushy eyebrows that moved up and down when he talked, a stutter when he was thinking, but a commanding and authoritative presence when he was preaching or lecturing. He wore ecclesiastical vestments well because he never looked pompous, only good humored. He could be both intimidating and warm and funny.

I came to know Michael Ramsey well after his retirement, when he would spend part of each year at Nashotah House, where I was teaching. When he was angry he could terrify both faculty and students; he once terrified me at dinner by questioning me rigorously about some work I was doing while he was tearing apart grilled shrimp. But most of the time he was a benign and pastoral person, always ready to take a walk or talk theology or simply be a friend to someone with a problem. He was greatly loved by us all, but we also stood in awe of so great a person.

And he was a great person not only because of his charismatic and sometimes eccentric personality but even more because of what he stood for and what he had accomplished in his time as a priest, bishop, and archbishop in the Anglican Communion. He was a theologian, a disciplined lover of Holy Scripture, a teacher and preacher of power, a pastor, and a person of deep spirituality. He was a prominent ecumenist, moving Anglicanism into closer relations with the Roman Catholic Church, the Orthodox, and the churches of the Reformation; he spoke forcefully on issues of social justice both in Britain and throughout the Anglican Communion; he presided over the church during the turbulent sixties; and he wrote important books and gave lectures to widely diverse audiences. And through it all he prayed and worshiped, and it was obvious to all who knew him that his praying and worshiping shaped everything else he did.

Michael Ramsey was born in 1904, in Cambridge, to a bookish and academic family. Following his education at the University of Cambridge, he was ordained in the Church of England and followed the upward path in the church that was customary in those days for a brilliant man: a brief curacy, a teacher of theology at a theological college, Canon and Professor of Divinity at Durham, Regius Professor of Divinity at Cambridge, Bishop of Durham, Archbishop of York, and finally Archbishop of Canterbury, Primate of All England and spiritual head of the Anglican Communion.

Throughout his ecclesiastical career he wrote and lectured extensively on theological subjects as well as on the pastoral issues that concerned clergy and lay people. He was not an original or ground-breaking theologian; in most of his writings he drew upon the usual Anglican sources in scripture, the church fathers, and Anglican divines. His more pastoral writings usually derived from addresses to church groups. Toward the end of his life he brought together his life of prayer in the small book *Be Still and Know*, which has become something of a classic in spiritual writings. His three major books on theological subjects were *The Gospel and the Catholic Church*, written while he was at Lincoln; *The Glory of God and the Transfiguration of Christ* (1949); and *From Gore to Temple: The Development of Anglican Theology between Lux Mundi and the Second World War* (published in the United States as *An Era in Anglican Theology*).

Of these major books, two are especially important. *The Gospel and the Catholic Church* contains themes which were to remain constant in Ramsey's theological work: the centrality of the cross for any understanding of the church, and his appeal to Scripture and tradition as a way forward, rather than as an archeological dig. The book was written during a time when much continental theology (except for Karl Barth) was under the sway of a liberalism which questioned the authority of Scripture and tradition. The book was a beginning of the kind of ecumenical theology that was to remain constant in his thinking: no work for unity has value unless grounded in Christian truth.

An Era in Anglican Theology was based upon a series of lectures which he gave for the Hale Foundation at Seabury-Western Seminary in 1959. The story is told (as far as I can remember, by Ramsey himself) that the title was changed because the American publisher thought that *From Gore to Temple* might suggest to American readers who were unfamiliar with the two great English theologians of the twentieth century a study of sacrifice in the Old Testament. It is Ramsey's major historical work, and is a magisterial study of theological developments with which he was deeply familiar, having himself come from the tradition of *Lux Mundi* and having known or studied with many of those with whom the book deals. The volume is essential for understanding the tensions in contemporary Anglicanism both in Britain and the United States: the struggles over biblical authority, the church's involvement in political and cultural movements, and our recognition of the importance of history in doctrinal development.

Throughout these major books and in his more occasional writings as well, there was a constant theme: the incarnation of God in Christ and the call of human beings through the incarnation into the glory of God. Why that theme remained central throughout all of his writings can best be understood from a brief recounting of his theological development.

Ramsey's approach to theology was a reflection of the state of theology itself in the Church of England in the early decades of this century; that he was able to expand and enrich his way of dealing with theological questions reflects his personal growth as a result of his increased responsibility as Archbishop of Canterbury and leader of the Anglican Communion. He began his theological work within the somewhat narrow confines of "English Anglicanism," represented by the writings of the Anglican divines and Richard Hooker's *Laws of Ecclesiastical Polity* from the sixteenth century. He was also influenced by the writings of the Oxford Movement of the nineteenth century; his reading of F. D. Maurice; his years of study under the New Testament scholar Sir Edwyn Hoskins; and his admiration for B. F. Westcott, the New Testament scholar and an earlier Bishop of Durham, and William Temple, theologian, political activist, and ecumenist who had also been Archbishop of Canterbury.

All of them had developed a peculiarly Anglican understanding of the doctrine of the incarnation as the foundation for interpreting the world, the church, and the sacramental life. For Ramsey, it was this heritage which expressed Anglicanism at its best: catholic and reformed, deeply aware of the human condition while yet worshiping the transcendent God, and a personal spirituality centered upon the eucharist as the way for human beings to enter into relationship with God. One of the selections from his early article "What is Anglican Theology?" (III, 10) that I have included in this volume expresses this heritage especially well: the catholicity and wholeness of Anglicanism is expressed in its recognition of human need and the sanctification of human life through sharing in the divine life.

At the same time, however, Ramsey was also aware of the limitations of such an incarnational theology: its tendency toward an optimism about the human condition and its forgetfulness of the sin and tragedy of life. In his first major book, *The Gospel and the Catholic Church,* he drew upon the theological work of the reformed theologian Karl Barth, whose emphasis on the cross and the need of redemption led Ramsey then and later in his life to stress the cross as the way to life in God. The resurrection without the cross, he always maintained, was meaningless. Incarnation and the sacramental life, with their call to participation in the life of God, need the corrective of redemption and repentance from sin.

Ramsey never pursued his initial interest in Barth; in fact, he was somewhat critical of Barth's theology of creation. However, it was this early influence, I believe, which enabled him to move beyond the facile optimism for which he criticized the liberalism of pre-World War II theology in his lectures on Anglican theology in *From Gore to Temple/An Era in Anglican Theology*. When he became Archbishop of Canterbury in 1961, Ramsey was confronted with a dramatically changed world and church from that in which he had grown up. The "Pax Britannia" had clearly ended, but so also had the society in which the Christian church, and especially the Church of England, was at the center. Archbishop Ramsey had to deal with questions which Professor Ramsey, and even Bishop Ramsey, would never have thought possible: nationalism and the emergence of a vital Anglicanism in the former British colonies; social and political questions about sexuality, class struggles, issues of life and death; and, most of all, a secularism which did not look favorably upon the past and its authority for contemporary life.

Archbishop Ramsey had to struggle with all those questions and many others, both in Britain and in his frequent travels throughout the Anglican Communion, as well as in his meetings with political leaders and the heads of other churches. Even though he hated ecumenical meetings (because, he said, they involved too much talk and too little serious thinking), he was involved in the World Council of Churches and its concern for justice and peace. He met with Pope Paul VI, with Orthodox prelates, and with leaders of various Protestant churches. He wrote in response to new trends in theology, although he later confessed that he was not happy with his somewhat negative response to Bishop J. A. T. Robinson's *Honest to God,* a small and very popular book published in the sixties that called for new ways of thinking about God, morality, and the Bible. He continued to teach what he believed to be the deep things of Christian faith: God, Christ, the Holy Spirit, the life of prayer, and the renewal of human society. Some of those writings are included in this volume.

As I have said, Bishop Ramsey was not an original or ground-breaking theologian. He was, however, a Christian who struggled to live out his relationship with God in the world of human affairs. He was not always successful in doing so, but his struggle provides deep insights into the struggle of all Christian people "to be with God" and to face honestly and courageously the glory and the sin of human beings.

He found the strength to do all that he did through the worship of the Christian community as he knew it in Anglicanism and through personal prayer. At Nashotah House, life centered around the chapel, with morning prayer, evensong, and the eucharist daily. Michael Ramsey was always in his place, and one could say, I hope without being sentimental, that his presence in worship was dynamic; it had a power which was palpable. On one occasion, he said to me that he spent more time getting ready to pray than actually praying. I took this to mean that he knew that all of the work he did was essential to his praying. For Michael Ramsey, the Christian hope was summed up in the notion of "wholeness": his belief that transfigured lives come about through work—both the tedious and the exciting—which is centered in God through worship and prayer.

It is very fitting that the engraving upon his tomb in Canterbury Cathedral (where he is buried next to William Temple) describes him as "Scholar, Priest and Friend" and ends with one of his favorite sayings from St. Irenaeus:

The Glory of God is the living man;
And the life of man is the Vision of God.

James E. Griffiss
Pentecost 1996

I

TEACHING THE
CHRISTIAN FAITH

Michael Ramsey understood his work as a bishop and later as an archbishop to be first and foremost that of a teacher of the Christian faith. When he was a diocesan bishop his pastoral addresses to his clergy were always serious; they dealt with theological questions of importance to the church or the nation. Later, as Archbishop of Canterbury, he saw himself as a more universal teacher for the Anglican Communion.

In the selections that follow he is concerned to teach about the foundation of the Christian church: its belief in God and in Jesus Christ—God first and God always. In order to teach that foundation he turns, as he so often did, to the Bible, as the source for Christian belief in God. There, Christians can be shown the God who is revealed in Jesus Christ; and there, also, the church can find its true vocation as a believing, worshiping, and serving community. Bishop Ramsey believed that only as the church preached and witnessed to God and to Jesus Christ crucified and risen would it be relevant to a confused and neglectful society.

~: **1** ~

The Future of the Christian Church

From *The Future of the Christian Church*, pp. 37-47.

In our thoughts about the future of the Christian church, we need to set the matter in the context of our faith in God. We say in the creed, "I believe in one Holy, Catholic, and Apostolic Church," and in so doing we affirm that the church is a part of "the faith" in which we believe. It is made by God, given by God. We value the sacraments and the ministerial order of the church as signs of the givenness of the church in history, of the meaning of the church as a sacrament of the eternal in the midst of time.

Yet we know that this divine gift is mediated through frail, sinful, and fallible men and women. The church is human as well as divine. It is divine because the principle of its life is the risen Lord present in his Body through the Holy Spirit. It is human inasmuch as its members are capable of sins and failings which grievously thwart and hinder the divine life within it. Hence in history the divine judgment again and again falls upon the church in its human part, and exhibits its members as what the prophets of old called "a hissing and a reproach." Yet again and again after a time of judgment, God has raised up a remnant of faithful people and used them for the execution of his purpose. It is in virtue, not of any quality inherent in the church's members, but of God's faithfulness in judging and raising up, that the church continues and "the gates of death shall not prevail against it."...

When therefore we say that we believe in the church, we do so only and always in terms of our belief in the God who judges and raises up. The mistake of ecclesiasticism through the ages has been to believe in the church as a kind of thing-in-itself. The apostles never regarded the church as a thing-in-itself. Their faith was in God, who had raised Jesus from the dead, and they knew the power of his resurrection to be at work in them and in their fellow believers despite the unworthiness of them all. This is always the true nature of belief in the church. It is a laying-hold on the power of the resurrection. And because it is that, it is always on the converse side *death:* death to self; death to worldly hopes; death to self-sufficiency; death to any kind of security for the church or for Christianity, other than the security of God and the resurrection.

We say this. We think we know this. But again and again we lapse into trying to make the church credible on grounds other than those of the God of the cross and the resurrection. We try to find the church's security, and our own security in the church, in false ways. I think of three familiar ways of false security: there are the false security of religion, the false security of theology, the false security of activism.

There is the false security of religion. We have had in the West much "religious prosperity": large congregations, devotional fervor, lovely music, the enjoyment of a genuine religious culture. This may be a true and authentic outcome of the gospel. Yet it may become a self-contained realm and with it there may be the tacit acceptance of assumptions about human society which are not those of the New Testament. So secure may religion feel itself that it may run on for long periods without criticizing itself, without submitting itself to the judgment of the gospel. And the genuine Christian virtues it produces may make it the more blind in its security. Then the draft comes. It came in England several decades ago. It is perhaps beginning to come in America today. When it comes, our religious security begins to fail us. We discover what F. D. Maurice meant when he said, "We have been dosing our people with religion, when what they want is not that but the living God."

If we are aware that this is our situation, what do we do? Too often we clutch at our religious security and try to refurbish it and protect it. But what ought we to do? We ought to suspect that God's judgment is falling on us, to try to discover why, and to look for our security to the God who, ever faithful to his church, exposes painfully, judges, and raises up.

Then, there is the false security of theology in the church. Now theology is a precious gift and God gave it. Theology is indispensable for the church and for every member of the church. But the object of faith is not theology but the God whose theology it is. We can be sound in the theology of the Bible, grasping correctly the biblical words and the biblical thought-forms....Yet our biblical theology can be held in a kind of vacuum, without sensitivity to the human context in which theology comes alive. So too, it can be used as a thing for the mind, without the knowledge that comes through prayer and contemplation. In those ways theology, divorced both from the social context and from the inner life, can become a thing-in-itself, and be substituted for the God who gave it. The substitution can be made equally by Barthians and by Liberals, by Catholics and by Protestants, each after his own kind.

When that happens, there comes a time of sickness and deadness in theology and people can begin to talk about God being dead. What then? The way of faith is not to try to bolster up old theology in the old ways, nor is it to abandon theology in the quest of a kind of Godless Christianity. The way of faith is rather to go into the darkness without fearing, and in the darkness to meet again the God who judges and raises from the dead.

Then, there is the false security of practical good works in the church. Now good works are the urgent outcome of faith and the lack of them may be often an occasion for divine judgment on the church. There can be no true faith which does not overflow in actions of compassion and human reconciliation. The church must be the servant of humanity. But woe to the church if it thinks it can justify itself to the world, and find its own security in a successful program of philanthropy. It was such a justification of his own mission which our Lord decisively rejected as he moved towards the cross for which he had been sent for the world's redemption. The church is called to serve without ceasing, but never to commend itself to the world by providing what the world would most like and approve on the world's own terms. When the church tries to commend itself in this way it can do good, it can win admiration for a while, but it can lose the power to lead people to repentance, to divine forgiveness, and to the God of the resurrection.

These forms of false security are familiar: security by religion, security by theology, security by activism. The pendulum sometimes swings between them. Not for a moment dare we belittle religion, for it is the creature's communion with the Creator; or theology, for it is the truth of God's word; or good works, for without them faith is dead. But each is God's gift, and not itself the end of faith. Our faith is in GOD, a faith that is always on one side frailty, self-distrust, penitence, death; and on the other side power, glory, resurrection. When times of leanness come we shall put ourselves under God's judgment and ask that our religion, our theology, our good works, and we ourselves may be humbled and cleansed. Then into the darkness the light of resurrection breaks. We cease to be confident and complacent about our religion, but we begin to pray with the awe and humility of children. We are less proud of our theology, but we allow the Word of God to find us in new and unexpected ways. We cease to commend our activism, but we spend ourselves in serving with the mind of unprofitable servants. The difference is that God is alive for us, and we now help other people to find God alive for them....

Faith means to look for no security in oneself, no security in one's fellow Christians, no security in any of the world's props or in any of the church's props, but security only in a nearness to the cross and to the resurrection beyond it. Such is the God in whom Christians believe; such is the church with the light of Calvary and Easter upon it.

It is in the midst of such a faith that we cherish our hopes about the church's future. What hopes does the New Testament encourage us to have?

The hope that rings through the apostolic writings is primarily the hope of the vision of God in heaven, the hope of the coming of Christ in glory, the hope also of the coming of the reign of God. "Come, Lord Jesus." The church worships, serves, preaches the gospel, draws men and women into fellowship with God, with its hope set not upon its own destiny but upon its Lord as it awaits his coming. Yet in one of the apostolic writings, the epistle to the Ephesians, the hope is in a measure focused upon the church itself, as Christ's Body and Christ's fullness; and the hope is that its members will grow into the completeness of his humanity, that humankind will be united in his Body and that the church, as Christ's bride, will be found without spot or wrinkle. Such then will be our hopes for the church, subordinate always to the hope for heaven and the hope for the coming of Christ.

We need, however, to remind ourselves that the New Testament, while it bids us hope firmly and hope joyfully, nowhere encourages us to expect that the coming of the kingdom of God will happen in a steady progression. It was indeed characteristic of much theology in the last century and the early years of the present century to think of the kingdom of God in that way. Humankind would become gradually more religious, more ethical in its behavior, more educated, more just in its social and economic life and so, through the steady growth of religion and knowledge, the kingdom of God would come. But neither our Lord nor the apostles encourage such an idea; rather, parts of their teaching suggest that there may be a series of catastrophic happenings in which evil shows itself with new power and, perhaps, there will be a final manifestation of evil in horrible forms, before Christ finally triumphs. To say this is not to lessen the confidence of the Christian hope, it is only to insist that it is always hope in the God of Calvary and Easter.

Nor does the New Testament encourage us to suppose that if only the church were really Christlike and really efficient in doing its work then people everywhere would be readily converted. The "if only" idea can be very misleading. We dare not overlook the words of St. Paul: "If our gospel is veiled it is veiled to those who are perishing. In their case the God of this world has blinded the minds of the unbelieving to keep them from seeing the light of the gospel of the glory of God in the face of Jesus Christ" (2 Cor. 4:3-4). The simplicity of the gospel does not mean that it can be easily grasped by those who are worldly and impenitent. It means that it poses the issue in a sharp and simple way and, in so doing, it divides humankind. At present, because the church is not Christlike enough, the division is often at the wrong line: there are some inside the church who would be outside the church if the church were more Christlike, and there are some outside the church who would be drawn inside if it were a more Christlike church. If the church bore its witness more faithfully, certain issues would be seen more sharply and simply.

The church will not be afraid to be a force which divides as well as unites, if its faith in God is sure. Faith will open our eyes to the presence of God in unsuspected ways. In the secular world and in the technological sciences God may be there, there to show us new apprehensions of himself and to give us new tasks to do. In the darkness of contemporary perplexities of thought God may be there, there to show us through darkness a new grasp of himself. In the sufferings of our fellows God may be there, there for us to serve him in Christ's brothers and sisters. In the catastrophes of the world God may be there, there in judgment to show human-kind the outcome of its own evil choices. And in the joy and serenity of those who serve him in faith, God may be there, the giver of a joy from heaven and a peace which surpasses every human contrivance.

In all these ways the perplexities that confront us are so many opportunities for faith to show itself. But to learn of God in new ways is not to abandon those that are old, if their claim rests not upon their being old but upon their being timeless. The worship and contemplation of God belong not to our immaturity but to our timeless privilege as God's children and creatures with heaven as our goal. And the sacrament of the body and blood of Christ in the eucharist belongs to the timeless participation of Christians in his death and resurrection. There the church renews its faith in the God who is true and living.

⌐ **2** ⌐

The God We Preach

From *The Christian Priest Today*, pp. 23-26.

We are challenged by [a malaise about faith in God] to renew our own knowledge of the living God of the Bible. He is the God of all creation, and not the God of religion alone. He is the God for whom none of the traditional images are adequate, and all of them are necessary to convey a reality greater than themselves. He is the God who has not deserted the world, but is here in judgment.

What then will you do about all this within your own ministry? It is one thing to discuss these great themes in an academic way, but how do they bear upon our day-to-day pastoral and teaching ministry? Let me make a few practical suggestions.

First, you will remember that nothing that is human and nothing that is created lies outside the compassion of God. You will care about people for themselves, and be interested in them for themselves, and not only as potential confirmation candidates. To have a solely religious interest in people is not only to be a bad pastor, it is also to be turning the true God into a sickly caricature of himself. Similarly, you will be concerned about the tremendous issues of the world we live in: poverty, affluence, pollution, race, war, violence, revolution. It is not that you will know the solution of these matters, or will make them the stock-in-trade of your preaching. It is rather that by your concern you will be sensitive to God's own concern, and so your thought about God will be nearer to the truth of his righteousness as a faithful creator. Through our concern about the world in which God is present in judgment and in mercy we learn to be in touch with the true God when we meet God in the church and in the sacraments.

Second, in using the historic imagery about God—imagery which is likely always to be with us—be very tender towards the simple, unquestioning piety of those who picture, believe, pray, and ask no questions. But with that tenderness combine a readiness to be often asking, gently of others and severely of oneself, "What are we really saying?"; "What do we really mean?" It is in the asking and the answering that faith becomes lively. To say that God is high above us is to say that we depend upon him as our creator, and that his holiness is beyond compare. And in what sense is God our Father? To let it be thought that he is just like your father or my father may cause more misunderstanding than light. It is the complacent failure of the Christian teacher to ask these questions which can allow people to drift into a faith which seems secure but is really rather sick.

I am sure too that, in talking with those who are not professed theists and yet are friendly and questioning, it is well sometimes to start not at our end but at theirs. If a person does not say "God," what does he or she say? What are those values or imperatives or absolutes, within the person and beyond, which signify most for him or her? It sometimes happens that such a discussion may reach a point where one is saying: "That is how you speak; it is not far from what we Christians mean by *God* or *grace.*"

Third, the recovery of the doctrine of the divine judgment is a direct appeal to biblical truth. But let the appeal be to the whole of the biblical concept, adumbrated in the Psalms and maturely gathered up in St. John. The supreme act of the divine judgment is the coming of Christ: "and this is the judgment, that the light is come into the world, and men loved the darkness rather than the light for their deeds were evil." It must be in the figure of Jesus crucified and risen that we present the divine judgment and the divine mercy. I see no other way of bringing the themes of sovereignty, power, compassion, judgment, home to our contemporaries except in terms of Jesus, in whom these divine actions are focused.

Let me add one final counsel. Beware of attitudes which try to make God smaller than the God who has revealed himself to us in Jesus. Let me illustrate what I mean.

Whenever exponents of the Christian faith treat it as something which we have to "defend" like a beleaguered fortress or a fragile structure they are making God to be smaller that he is. There is the idea that the greatness of the God of the Bible is protected by a kind of defensive literalism which insists on the historicity of the narratives and supposes that to waver on the Mosaic authorship of the Pentateuch or the sojourn of Jonah in the whale is to make grievous concessions to modern secularism. But the God of the Bible is majestic enough not to require such protection, as he is able to use in his scriptures not only literal history but poetry, drama, myth, and symbol also in conveying his truth to humankind.

There is also a kind of defensive Catholicism which supposes that no risks must be taken in the process of Christian unity, as if Catholic truth needed "protecting," whereas the gifts of God are powerful enough to vindicate themselves in the growing together of different traditions. The truth of God is greater than our efforts to conserve it.

So too there is a spirit of fearfulness which thinks that no good can ever come of movements which are outside the camp of Christendom, forgetting that God could use a Cyrus, an Assyria, or an altar to an unknown deity in his great purpose in history. We are not indeed to confuse what God does as redeemer in the unique sphere of gospel and church with what he does as illuminator through the light that lighteth everyone; but to be blind to the latter is not to enhance the former or to understand it better.

One more instance. There are those who, eager to respect the contemporary mind and the claims of reason, try to deny to God anything which seems to be beyond the contemporary grasp or rational apprehension. To do this is to miss that God's thoughts are not our thoughts nor God's ways our ways, and that eye has not seen, ear has not heard, nor has it entered into our hearts to conceive what God has prepared for them that love him. Such is the God whom we preach, and the need for him today is as desperate as it ever was.

❧ 3 ❧

Word and Preacher

From *Durham Essays*, pp. 22-28.

My purpose is to ask you to consider the theology of the Word in its bearing upon the task of the Christian preacher. Most of us can recall debates as to whether the Bible is the Word of God or contains the Word of God; but what matters supremely is not which lobby we vote in upon that somewhat inconclusive question, but our fidelity to the *conception* of the divine Word which the Bible presents to us.

The God of the Bible is from first to last a God who speaks. This does not mean primarily that he is One who provides humankind with auditions, voices, oracles, and similar "experiences"; nor does it mean that he is one to whom it is proper to attribute speech rather than action. It means that God is ceaselessly active, and that all his activity involves a relationship to his creatures which is akin to speech. In the creation of the world, in the sustaining of the world and all that it contains, in the providential government of nature and history, in the direction of the movement of events with their calamities and deliverances, God "speaks," both in the sense that what happens is wrought by his command, and in the sense that what happens has itself the nature of a voice—whether of command or challenge or summons or consolation—to the human observer. In all that God does there is the incisiveness which we connect in speech with the imperative mood, in common life with a sharp knife. Nowhere is this better expressed than in the Book of Wisdom:

> For while peaceful silence enwrapped all things, and night in her own swiftness was in mid course, thine all-powerful word leaped from heaven out of the royal throne, a stern warrior, into the midst of the doomed land, bearing as a sharp sword thine unfeigned commandment. (Wisd. 18:14-16)

Or, in the epistle to the Hebrews:

> For the word of God is living, and active, and sharper than any two-edged sword, and piercing even to the dividing of soul and spirit, of both joints and marrow, and quick to discern the thoughts and intents of the heart. (Heb. 4:12)

This dynamic, incisive, challenging note belongs to all the divine activity in creation, in providence, and in the incarnation of the Word made flesh.

Nothing less than this is the background to Christian preaching. The Word whom we preach is the Word who created the world, who sustains its order and beauty, who is ever at work in the ups and downs of history, whose coming in Jesus is the key to the whole. To the preacher the realization of this is at once shattering and consoling; shattering because the preacher's theme is so vast, consoling because behind all preachers is the almighty action of God in all things, and they are called not to be wise or powerful themselves but to bid their hearers hearken to what God is saying in God's own ceaseless action in the world. The Word is not imprisoned in the sermon; for it is present in its sovereign power before the preacher's mouth is opened and after the preacher's lips are closed.

So much for the general character of the doctrine of the Word. Now I would ask you to consider some different uses of the term *logos* in the New Testament, for they suggest to us different aspects of the business of the preacher.

1. First, there are the *logoi*, the words or sayings spoken by our Lord, and preserved in the early church....

2. Then, there is the *logos* in the sense of the message spoken by Jesus Christ considered as a whole....

3. Thirdly, there is the *logos* as the message about Christ, or God in Christ, preached by the apostles after the mission of Christ was consummated....

4. Lastly, there is the *logos* meaning the Person of the Lord himself, the eternal Word now made flesh....

These four uses of the word *logos* suggest therefore four factors in the preacher's material. There are the sayings of Jesus; the preacher recalls these and brings their dynamic authority home to his or her hearers. There is the message and teaching of Jesus as a whole; and the preacher tries to be faithful to its content and method, not forgetting its many facets—the severity and the tenderness, the homeliness and the otherworldliness, the stern demands of moral surrender and the graciousness which makes demand always to be pervaded by gift, sheer gratuitous gift. Then there are the events which the apostles preached; Bethlehem, Calvary, the Empty Tomb. And finally there is Jesus himself; to the preacher there sometimes happens that miracle of grace whereby Jesus himself is made known and accessible—not statements about him, but himself the name above every name.

It is not difficult for us to recall lopsided phases in Christian preaching—perhaps in our own—when the concentration on one of these elements has gone with a disastrous neglect of the others. The first two in isolation may give us a Galilean gospel falsely abstracted from its climax in the *Via Crucis*. The third (which is indeed central and cardinal) may, when isolated from the first two, give us a dogmatic gospel of the Lord's death and resurrection disconnected—like a sort of evangelical mystery religion—from the ethical context of the life and words of the Son of Man. The fourth, whenever we treat it in a facile way as if it did not involve the discipline of the others, can suggest the sentimental and unreal preaching of "Jesus only" which has shirked those hard paradoxes of history and dogma wherein the claim of Jesus lies.

I now go on to ask whether these different aspects of the preacher's task and material do not suggest to us different types of sermons on our part, or rather different uses of scripture and of "the text" within the sermon.

1. *The sayings of Christ.*
When we are preaching about this, we shall let the particular saying dominate the sermon. Our aim is to bring the saying home in its dynamic authority. We therefore picture to our hearers the setting and the scene in the gospel story, and try to lead our hearers to see themselves there and find the saying in its majestic force pricking their consciences and illuminating their minds. If, for instance, the theme is the word to the paralytic, "Son, thy sins be forgiven thee," the hearers may be helped to see themselves alongside the paralytic and to hear Christ's word addressed to their need as to his. The text, and its setting, will dominate.

2. *The teaching of Christ in its broader, comprehensive themes.*
If the sermon sets itself to draw out some aspect of this, then the text may not have the same relation to the sermon. The text illustrates a theme, in expounding which the preacher may move about the gospels. For instance, the text "My kingdom is not of this world" might be used not only to draw out the issue of Christ before Pilate, but as a pointer for a treatment of the otherworldliness of the kingdom of God, which might indeed begin with the temptations in the wilderness and move on to the passion and beyond.

3. *The evangelical events as the sum of the apostolic gospel.*
Here the sermon is doing something different from either of the former kinds we have considered. Its subject is an event, a mystery of the faith, such as Bethlehem, Calvary, the risen Lord. The text here may be neither a saying in its own context nor the peg for a theme of teaching, but rather a kind of mirror of one of the mysteries of the faith. "They found the babe lying in a manger"; here is mirrored the dogma of the Eternal God made Man. "He was reckoned with the transgressors"; here is mirrored the Sinless One suffering for sinners. The preacher uses the text to lead the hearers to gaze upon one of the great mysteries of God.

4. The Word as meaning Jesus himself.
What use of text or scripture, or what kind of sermon, here corresponds? "Sir, we would see Jesus." Here no technique, no categorization aids us. It happens that sometimes there comes that costly simplicity whereby the person of the Lord becomes vivid, piercing to the dividing of bone and marrow.

Let me not suggest that the four factors in the New Testament conception correspond directly or self-consciously with four kinds of sermons. That would be altogether an oversimplification. It seems, nonetheless, that the four factors demand expression in our preaching, and do suggest to us particular emphasis and ways of using scripture. Now I would rashly go a step further, and ask whether these different elements in our preaching do not call for different procedures in our *theological and biblical study.*

1. The words of Christ in their own scene and setting.
This sort of sermon demands that we study the passage in itself. The great commentaries have for this a special value. So have the *good* works on the life of our Lord. We need to get as far inside the gospel story as we can. But no less important is it that the saying is the saying of a Lord who is now living. Hence our study of the classical commentary will go hand-in-hand with our meditation upon our Lord's contemporary presence and sacramental gift. The words of Jesus are spirit and life, where Jesus is not merely a memory of the past, but One who is feeding our hearers with his flesh and blood.

2. The teaching of Christ in its comprehensive themes.
Here a different sort of biblical study is called for; not the exploration of the passage in itself with the concentration provided by the great commentary, but the tracing through many passages with concordance and other aid, of some of the great biblical words. The need for this kind of study has called forth a new kind of book, the *word-book,* where biblical terms are treated more fully than in a lexicon if less exhaustively than in a single volume upon each. Study of this kind equips us specially for the second of the factors in preaching of which we have been thinking.

3. The evangelical events, the saving mysteries.
Here exegesis passes into dogmatic theology. If preachers are awed by this, let them remember that dogmatic theology means only the asking and the answering of certain inevitable questions. This the preachers do. Entrusted to them is one of the great events of the gospel. They ask: why was this necessary? What does it tell us about God? about human beings? What did it cost? What effect did it have? What demands does it make? What gifts does it bring? Ask those questions, and you are talking dogmatic and ascetical and moral theology, and relating them to the plain business of any sermon upon the mysteries of the faith. The reading of the best works of dogmatic theology enables us to return refreshed to the exposition of the events wherein the dogmas are mirrored.

4. Study which relates to the preaching of Jesus in simplicity.
There is simplicity born of shallowness, and falsely so called; and there is a simplicity which is the costly outcome of the discipline of mind and heart and will. Simplicity in preaching is properly the simplicity of the knowledge of God and of human beings. To say of someone "this person preaches simply" is to say "this preacher walks with God."

I would return to pick up the point with which we began, that the Word whom we preach is the Word who is ever active in the created world. While therefore our message comes from another world and summons hearers to receive a gift which is utterly new and from above, it also interprets to them what is happening already in this world as the scene of divine mercy and judgment, and within themselves as creatures in whom is the divine image. The preacher will ask for a portion of that gift whereby the prophets could discern the hand of God in things contemporary, and of that reverence for men and women wherewith the Incarnate Lord showed to them the meaning of themselves. I am not sure whether what is sometimes rather self-consciously called "biblical preaching" always bears this in mind. If it is borne in mind, preaching will never mean the declaiming of biblical phrases into space, for it will contain something akin to the parabolic method of our Lord.

⌣ **4** ⌣

Preaching Jesus Today

From *The Christian Priest Today*, pp. 27-31.

Jesus Christ is himself the gospel which we preach (cf. Acts 5:42; 8:25; 11:20). He is himself the essence of the good news. I ask you to think about some of the formidable difficulties which confront us today as we set about the preaching of Jesus. I am not thinking only of our sermons, which are almost always addressed to those who are within the circle of faith, but of all that the church does to convey a message about Jesus, a message whose heart and center is Jesus.

There is first of all the difficulty of conveying a historical faith to people who, like so many of our contemporaries, are without any sense of history. True, we preach Jesus as living and contemporary, and we link the past history with his presence now in the eucharist. Yet our understanding of his character and message is derived from historical events which occurred nearly two thousand years ago. True, we say that God is living and active in the world today; yet we ascribe unique and revelatory importance to those things which we say God wrought through Jesus on the soil of Palestine in the time of Pontius Pilate. However contemporary we may try to be, our authority rests upon an "old, old story." And all this amid a generation for whom the sense of the past is very faint. I would say that one of the biggest differences between the up-and-coming generation in England and its predecessors is that it has a thick curtain between itself and past history or tradition. My own generation felt itself to belong to a stream which flowed through past time: this generation has its consciousness filled and absorbed by the present. The "secular" outlook, as we call it, means largely an outlook limited by the frontiers of the present *saeculum.*

Furthermore, where people *are* ready to be interested in the past they look at it with a more critical eye about its credibility, and it is felt that the history of Jesus of Nazareth is unsure. The impact of form-criticism has undermined the view that the gospels can be read as diary reminiscences and has set them in the context of the preaching, the worship, and the theologizing of the early church. Now we can say—and for my own part I do not hesitate to say—that the form-critical method need not involve historical scepticism. If the gospels give us interpretative portraits of Jesus painted within the post-resurrection church, the picture conveyed may be a true one if the interpretations are true, and we are shown Jesus as he was in his total impact upon his followers. We may be no less sure that it was not the church or the evangelists who created Jesus, but Jesus who created them.

Yet while we may ourselves feel assured about the sufficient historical basis of the gospel, there remains a feeling of remoteness between the gospels and the world in which people live today. Take the synoptic gospels. The narratives are full of miraculous happenings. We can expound and defend these in the context of the incarnation, and for my part I do not hesitate to do so. But our hearers may feel: "They may be true, but is this the world we live in?" And the teaching is full of apocalyptic imagery; to say that this of course needs interpretation and is not to be taken literally is to emphasize again the gap between the world of the gospels and the world of today. Fewer people today have the poetic feeling which builds an imaginative bridge from one culture to another. Because of the remoteness of the world view of the synoptists many modern readers more easily feel the timeless appeal of Jesus in the "universal" imagery of the Fourth Gospel: life, light, bread, water, door, way, truth, word; and the Johannine discourses reach across the centuries. But here too the problems of history raise their head.

Let me now suggest to you a way of approaching the problem of presenting Jesus Christ to our contemporaries. We start with those facts about him which very few would wish to deny.

First, Jesus of Nazareth, a prophet and a teacher, did exist. We can safely say that to deny this is a piece of historical eccentricity.

Next, Jesus of Nazareth died by crucifixion. Here too we are on unassailable ground.

Then, as a result of the career of Jesus of Nazareth there came into history the phenomenon of Christianity, the new movement with its society, its teaching, its rites, its doctrine, its ethics, its impact on the world, for better or for worse. This is again indisputable, whatever significance is ascribed to it and in whatever way the causal connection between Jesus and the church is traced.

So far we are on agreed ground. Now I take a further step and ask about the new phenomenon of Christianity and its character. Within this new phenomenon of Christianity there is a strikingly new valuation of suffering. This is seen in the teachings, the liturgies, the ethical attitudes, the view of the world, and the practical behavior of the Christians. The ignominious death by crucifixion which was meted out to Jesus is not shame and disgrace: it is "good news," it is of God, it has a victorious character. They are "glad to be counted worthy to suffer dishonor for the name" (Acts 5:41). They are in the midst of sufferings "more than conquerors" (Rom. 8:37).

Now we ask: If this be a significant part of the phenomenon of Christianity, what happened to bring it about? It is true that Jesus gave to his disciples a good deal of teaching about the meaning of his coming suffering and death, but this teaching did not apparently penetrate their minds. It baffled them, and when Jesus died the disciples had not learned the secret; indeed the secret died with him. Something *happened* to create for the disciples the new doctrine of the death as significant and victorious. I believe that the something which happened was the resurrection. The alternative theories, that the apostles were deceived or deceiving, or the victims of hallucination or wishful thinking, seem to me to call for an extreme kind of credulity, a credulity far removed from scientific history. I believe that there was an event, and that the apostles were right in their belief about it. Jesus had been raised from death.

We have often heard discussions about the sense in which the resurrection was "bodily" or "spiritual," and our understanding of those categories is far from adequate. I see as a very important characteristic of the resurrection, both in the gospel narratives and in the apostles' teaching, that it was the resurrection of *the crucified one:* it was the coming back to the disciples, and the making available to future generations, of *Jesus who died,* Jesus in his death. It is not that the death is an incident now left behind: no, the death is always with us, vindicated in its undying significance.

Not for nothing are the episodes in the gospel traditions where the wounds of the crucifixion are still visible when the risen Jesus appears. The risen Jesus is still the crucified one.

Here then is the central point of the history of Jesus. He was not a forgotten crucified teacher. His impact survived, and Christianity came into existence because the resurrection happened and because it was the resurrection of the crucified. And besides being the events which brought Christianity to birth, the death and resurrection are the events which characterize the nature of Christianity. It is a gospel of life through death, of losing life so as to find it. Thus the Christian's act of allegiance to the risen Lord Jesus was, and still is, an act of acceptance of the way of the cross. So too the act of faith in the Christian God is an act which sees the sacrifice of self right down to the point of death and destruction, and then says: This, and only this, is the sovereign power of God. In the imagery of the Apocalypse the lamb (self-sacrifice) and the throne (sovereignty) go together.

Crucifixion-resurrection was the core of the history with which the early church was concerned: it was this which was the center of the preaching and the liturgy. But here was no mere mystery religion of a dying and rising deity, for in the case of Jesus it mattered greatly who and of what sort was the One who thus died and rose again. How had he lived? What did he do, and what did he teach? So besides the story of Good Friday and Easter the church treasured the traditions about the words and the works of Jesus, and these traditions eventually came to be embodied in the written gospels.

Such is the approach to the history of Jesus which I suggest to you. I start with the very few data: that the history of Jesus was such as to account for the strikingly new and creative element in primitive Christianity. This gives the death and the resurrection as the central facts, and also as the heart of the interpretation of Jesus. Like Bultmann I see the act of faith in the risen Lord as faith in the supremacy of the cross: unlike him I am convinced that the resurrection was a historic event, acceptable on strong evidence, which gave to the cross its significance for the apostles. Unlike him also I believe that the early church was greatly interested in the life and teaching of Jesus for its own sake, always in the light of the central cross and resurrection faith.

I suggest to you that as the cross and the resurrection were the spearhead of the gospel's relevance and potency in the first century so they can be also for our contemporary world. Ours is a world full of suffering and frustration: of what significance to it is Jesus who lived and died nearly two thousand years ago? The answer is: chiefly in this, that in his death and resurrection he shows not only the way for men and women but the very image of God himself. Is there within or beyond our suffering and frustrated universe any purpose, way, meaning, sovereignty? We answer, yes, there is purpose, way, meaning, sovereignty, and the death and resurrection of Jesus portray it as living through dying, as losing self to find self, as the power of sacrificial love.

To commit oneself to this way is to be near to the secret of God's own sovereignty, near to the power which already wins victories over evil and will ultimately prevail. That is the point at which Jesus can be shown to be near to our own world; and when he is found to be near at this point then his life and teaching are found to have their compelling fascination. Through the life and the teaching there runs the principle "he who exalts himself shall be abased, and he who humbles himself shall be exalted." Through the life and teaching there is the strange blending of authority and humility.

So the church is called to be the fellowship of Christ crucified and risen. In the eucharist it proclaims Christ's death and feeds upon his life. We are familiar with this; but how tremendous are the implications. It implies a fellowship of Christians marked by an unselfish openness to one another in Christ's name, a like openness in the service of the community and a commitment to the way which led to Calvary. There are those who wonder whether the old institutional church can rise to this, its essential calling, and there are those who are finding the cross-resurrection commitment in ways outside the old institutions.

I suggest that here, however, is the point of impact of the old story of Jesus upon our new world: die to live. Here too is the meaning of the church, and the meaning of apostolic ministry: "always bearing about in the body the dying of Jesus, that the life also of Jesus may be manifested in our body" (2 Cor. 4:10).

II

THE CHURCH:
CRISIS IN CREDIBILITY

These selections are drawn from Michael Ramsey's first book, *The Gospel and the Catholic Church*, and from two of his writings after he had become Archbishop of Canterbury. In all three there is a common theme: how are we to talk about the church so that it can be seen by "the world" as something more than just another fractured and outdated institution? How can we talk about the church as a vital and dynamic presence in the world?

The Gospel and the Catholic Church sought to do this by returning to the biblical foundation of the church in the death and resurrection of Christ and by showing that all of the structures of the church, particularly its ministry, derive from Christ. The book was especially important because it got underneath the controversies which divided Christians: the church must always die and live with Christ, and its external structures must always bear witness to the crucified and risen Christ.

The other two selections show how Ramsey, much later in his life, was still concerned to show that the church always needed to return to the same foundation when it seemed to be losing its way in an increasingly secular world. Ramsey did not advocate a trivial or superficial "relevance" as an antidote to modern challenges. He believed that the *Gospel* had to be preached. But at the same time he knew that the Gospel had to be preached so that it could be heard by those who lived in the complexities of a secular world. Thus he came to a new appreciation of *Honest to God*, and he sought to show how the spiritual life cannot be in opposition to the material and secular world.

✣ 5 ✣

What is Truth?

From *The Gospel and the Catholic Church*, pp. 120-126.

Jesus Christ is not only the Way and the Life. He is also the Truth; and the church, which is his Body, is commissioned to teach the Truth. How shall the church know where to find what is true, and how, after finding it, shall the church assimilate it so as to proclaim it with authority?

The answer to these questions has, in Christian history, been sought specially in two phrases, "the authority of the Bible" and "the authority of the church." Some have turned to the Bible as a whole or to the New Testament, and have said in effect, "Propositions about God which we find here are true; those which we do not find here are unwarranted or false." Others have turned to the church as a divine institution and have said in effect, "This institution is divinely inspired. What it teaches *(semper et ubique et ab omnibus)* is true." We are not to say that either of these methods is wrong; but neither of them goes deep enough. The deeper questions are these. What does the Bible mean by "Truth"? What did our Lord mean when he said "I am the Truth"? and what does the word "truth" mean on the lips of the church's teachers? It is not enough, and it may be even misleading to assert that Truth is found in the Bible and in the church. We must ask, "What is this Truth which has created both the church and the Bible?"

In our quest of the meaning of "Truth" we shall start by examining the two words *aletheia* (truth) and *sophia* (wisdom) as used in the New Testament; and this examination will provide a basis for our consideration of the nature of Christian doctrine and the authority of the Christian church.

Aletheia

Aletheia is used in the Old Testament of God's *steadfastness* in providence and in redemption. The Truth is a quality of the living God in action (Pss. 100:5; 31:5; 85:10; and Micah 7:20). Thus the Truth is God's saving plan as he rules in history with righteous purpose. Karl Barth well reproduces the Old Testament meaning of "Truth" when he writes, "Truth is not what we think and say, but what God has done, will do, and is doing."[1] Such is the background to the word *aletheia* in the New Testament, and the same redemptive note is present in St. Paul's and in St. John's use of the word (Gal. 2:5, 14; Col. 1:5; Rom. 15:8; Eph. 1:13; 1 Tim. 2:3; 2 Tim. 2:25). Thus Truth is uttered in God's redemption through Christ, and Christians learn the Truth through repentance as well as through intellectual processes, and apprehend the Truth in their life as well as in their thinking (Eph. 4:24 and 6:14; 2 Thess. 2:13).

Nor is the teaching of St. John essentially different; the emphasis is upon the incarnation rather than upon the cross, but the redemptive note is present. "The word was made flesh and dwelt among us, and we beheld his glory,...full of grace and truth."...God's truth is not an abstract value to be contemplated; it is active to save in Christ. Christ is the Truth (John 14:6), God's word is Truth (17:17), and the disciple is the one who *does* the Truth (John 8:32). More, still, St. John links truth with the passion of our Lord (John 17:17-19). Crucifixion—Truth—the life of holiness, all these are linked....

In short, the Christian use of the word *aletheia* in the New Testament suggests that Truth centers in the redemptive death of Christ, and that it is learned in the common life of the society created by that death.

Sophia

The use of the word *sophia*, wisdom, in the New Testament is equally striking. Wisdom is an attribute of God himself (Rom. 11:33; Eph. 3:10; James 3:17). It is manifested in Christ, "in whom are all the treasures of wisdom and knowledge hidden" (Col. 2:3). Nay more, Christ is himself the Wisdom of God, for to him are

---

1. *Epistle to the Romans*, English trans., p. 301.

ascribed those functions of creating and sustaining the universe, ruling over history, and disclosing God's purpose to all, functions which belong to the Wisdom of God in the wisdom literature (1 Cor. 8:6, 10:4; Col. 1:16-17; cf. Prov. 8:22-36, Wisdom 7:22 ff.). And Wisdom is set forth in the death of Christ, in direct contrast to human wisdom and as the negation of the wisest ideas of the world (1 Cor. 1:18-23). It is shortly after this account of Wisdom disclosed by the cross that St. Paul passes on to describe the Wisdom which dwells in the Christians to whom the Spirit gives a knowledge of the things of God (1 Cor. 2:6-10).

Thus the Christians, brought into the Wisdom of the crucified, are led on to the life of Wisdom in the Spirit....The range of this Wisdom is as wide as the whole world, for the whole world, created by God, becomes intelligible in the light of the crucifixion wherein the character and method of divine government are disclosed. He who redeemed men and women is also he who created the world and in whom all things shall be summed up, and the fellowship which shares in death and resurrection shall be led by the Holy Spirit to interpret all life and all history. This work of interpretation involves all the activities of the human intellect and every part of science and art and research; yet the process of knowledge is not by these activities alone. For there are secrets of the meaning of the world that are unlocked through a knowledge which is linked with the life and love of the society that shares in the cross; a knowledge which grows through the building up of the one Body in love (Phil. 1:9; Eph. 4:13). Christian knowledge and Christian love lie close together, and Christian theology is not only a detached exercise of the Christian intellect; it is the life of the one Body in which Truth is both thought out and lived out.

In the light of the meaning of the words "Truth" and "Wisdom" in the New Testament the nature of the church's doctrine and authority becomes plain. These facts emerge inescapably from our biblical study.

First, the Wisdom of God is working through all created life, and far and wide is the sustainer and the inspirer of the thought and the endeavor of men and women. The church will therefore reverence every honest activity of their minds; it will perceive that therein the Spirit of God is moving, and it will tremble lest by denying this, in word or in action, it blaspheme the Spirit of God. But Wisdom cannot be thus learned in all its fullness. The mind and the eye of many are distorted by sin and self-worship; and the Wisdom which the Spirit of God unfolds throughout the world can lead to blindness and to deceit unless human beings face the fact of sin and the need for redemption.

Hence, the church proclaims the Wisdom of God, set forth in its very essence in the crucifixion of Jesus Christ, a Wisdom learned when men and women are brought to the crisis of repentance and to the resulting knowledge of self and of God. The Wisdom of the cross seems at first to deny the Wisdom of the Spirit of God in the created world; it scandalizes our sense of the good and the beautiful. But Christians, who have first faced the scandal, discover in the cross a key to the meaning of all creation. The cross unlocks its secrets and its sorrow, and interprets them in terms of the power of God.

Thus, the Wisdom uttered in the cross has created the church and is expressed through the church's whole life as the Body of Christ crucified and risen. The church's work in thinking and interpreting and teaching is inseparable from the church's life in Christ. Its authority is Christ himself, known in the building up of the one Body in truth and in love. Hence "orthodoxy" means not only "right opinion," but also "right worship" or "true glory," after the biblical meaning of the word *doxa;* for life and thought and worship are inseparable activities in the Body of Christ.

In these three ways the church will be faithful to the biblical meaning of Truth, by reverencing the works of God everywhere and the Spirit of God manifested in the endeavors of human minds; by keeping before itself and before men and women the scandal of the cross; and by remembering that orthodoxy means not only correct propositions about God, but the life of the one Body of Christ in the due working of all its members....

It follows that the church can never be said to have apprehended the Truth; rather, it is the Truth, the divine action, which apprehends the church. Dimly it understands what it teaches. For the more the church learns of God, the more it is aware of the incomprehensible mystery of his being, in creation and in transcendence and on the cross....

Ineffable, therefore, is the revelation of God, which creates and which uses the teaching church. Human language can never express it. Yet the church, like its Lord, must partly commit it to human speech and thought, and is indeed commissioned to do this in every age and civilization. Hence have appeared the canon of scripture and the creeds; both express and both control the church's teaching. But, since Truth and life and worship are inseparable, the scriptures and the creeds are not given for use in isolation. They form, with the ministry and the sacraments, one close-knit structure which points Christians to the historical facts wherein God is revealed, and to the life and experience of the universal society.

∾ 6 ∾

The Church and the Gospel

From *The Gospel and the Catholic Church*, pp. 3-9.

Throughout the centuries the church of God has had both its devoted adherents, who would die for it, and its persecutors, who have sought to destroy it. Thus, both in love and in hatred, people have reckoned with it seriously, and have been compelled to think out their attitude towards it. But at the present time there is a very different mood widespread, one of apathy and bewilderment which asks, "What is this strange thing, the Christian church? Whatever can it mean? What relation have its services, its hierarchy, its dogmas, its archaic and beautiful language, to the daily troubles of humankind?" This bewilderment leads many to pass the church by, since it seems to do and say so little about the things which matter supremely—world peace, social reform, the economic tangle. "And is not the church itself divided and beset with controversy?" Surrounded by people too apathetic even to be hostile, Christians are driven to think out where the relevance of the church really lies.

There are many, therefore, within the church who believe that its relevance must be found in its ability to take a lead in social and international policies, and who would meet the situation by attempts to make the church "up-to-date" and "broad-minded" and "progressive" in the cause of peace and economic reform. The church, in their view, must bestir itself to provide such remedies as thoughtful individuals outside the church demand, and to answer the questions which such people are asking; and if it fails to do this it remains a scandal, ignored by this generation.

But the New Testament suggests that the right answer begins at a very different point. For the relevance of the church of the apostles consisted not in the provision of outward peace for the nations, nor in the direct removal of social distress, nor yet in any outward beauty of the church itself, but in pointing to the death of Jesus the Messiah, and to the deeper issues of sin and judgment—sin in which the Christians had shared, judgment under which they stood together with the rest of humankind. In all this the church was scandalous and unintelligible, but by all this and by nothing else it was relevant to their deepest needs.

For the relevance of the church can never be any easier than was the relevance of the Messiah. He provoked questionings and doubts among many of the wisest and holiest of his race. He perplexed those who looked to him as a national leader, as a reformer, a prophet, a teacher, and a healer, and even as Messiah; for he abandoned his useful and intelligible works in Galilee in order to bring God's kingdom by dying on the cross. "There was no beauty in him that we should desire him." And the life beset by the "whys?" and the "wherefores?" of good and sensible people ended with the terrible question mark of the cry of desolation from the cross, "My God, my God, why hast thou forsaken me?" So ended his earthly life, but in the manner of its end and in the "why?" uttered on Calvary, there was present the power of God; for Jesus knew whence he came and whither he was going.

His church on earth is scandalous, with the question marks set against it by bewildered men and women and with the question mark of Calvary at the center of its teaching; yet precisely there is the power of God found, if only the Christians know whence they come and whither they go. They are sent to be the place where the passion of Jesus Christ is known and where witness is borne to the resurrection from the dead. Hence the philanthropist, the reformer, the broad-minded modern person can never understand, in terms of their own ideals, what the church is or what it means. Of course it is scandalous, of course it is formed of sinners whose sinfulness is exposed by the light of the cross, of course there is an awful question mark at its center. These things must needs be, if it is the Body of Christ crucified and risen from the dead.

Thus the first need of Christians, in face of the apathy and the bewilderment about the church, is to know and to be able to say plainly what the church really *is*. This does not mean to know and to say what the church *ought* to be—that it ought to be full of love and peace and to shower blessings on humankind, and that it will soon be doing this through a new energy of the Holy Spirit. "It doth not yet appear what we shall be." Before Christians can say these things about what the church ought to be, their first need is to say what the church is, here and now amid its own failures and the questionings of the bewildered.

Looking at it now, with its inconsistencies and its perversions and its want of perfection, we must ask what is the real meaning of it just as it is. As the eye gazes upon it, it sees—the passion of Jesus Christ. And the eye of faith sees further—the power of Almighty God. The Christians will not try to answer the philanthropist and the reformer by meeting them on their own terms and by hiding the scandalous gospel. They will say plainly what the church of God is, and whither it points. Philanthropies point to the conditions of human lives, the church points to the deeper problem of men and women themselves....

The theologian is forced by the New Testament to study the church [in terms of the gospel of Christ crucified and risen]. The church has often been expounded as the "extension of the incarnation," and in these terms some classical teaching about the church has been given. But the New Testament takes us deeper than this. It shows us how the disciples knew themselves to be the refounded Israel of God through being partakers in the Messiah's death. The prediction by Jesus of his death had bewildered them; and in answer to their bewilderment he taught them that they would not understand the death except by sharing in it....Before ever the apostles realized the full doctrine of the incarnation or thought of the church in terms of it, they knew the church through knowing the Lord's death and resurrection. Thus, while it is true that the church is founded upon the Word-made-flesh, it is true only because the Word was identified with human beings right down to the point of death, and enabled them to find unity through a veritable death to self.

The doctrine of the church, and its order, ministry, and sacraments [must be] expounded not primarily in terms of an institution founded by Christ, but in terms of Christ's death and resurrection, of which the one Body, with its life and its order, is the expression.

The movement towards the *reunion* of Christendom is also compelled to see its problems in close connection with the Christ's passion. Before they pass on to their schemes of reconciliation, Christians are compelled to pause and ask what the present fact of disunity means. Why is it? And they will not simply say that it is wrong, and flee from it in the quest of new visions and ideals and policies; they will pause again and dwell upon the facts, just as they are. In them is the passion of Jesus; and in them already the power of God. Both divisions and unity remind us of the death and resurrection of Jesus. Division severs his body: but unity means the one Body, in which every member and every local community dies to self in its utter dependence upon the whole, the structure of the Body thereby setting forth the dying and rising with Christ. And if the problems about schism and reunion mean dying and rising with Christ, they will not be solved through easy humanistic ideas of fellowship and brotherhood, but by the hard road of the cross.

When reunion has been discussed, there has often seemed to be an impasse between two types of Christianity. On the one hand, there is the Catholic tradition which thinks of the church as a divine institution, the gift of God to human beings, and which emphasizes outward order and continuity and the validity of its ministry and sacraments. To the exponents of this tradition, unity is inconceivable apart from the historic structure of the church. On the other hand, there is the Evangelical tradition which sees the divine gift not in the institution but in the gospel of God, and which thinks less of church order than of the Word of God and of justification by faith. This tradition indeed emphasizes the divine society of the redeemed, but it finds it hard to understand the Catholic's thought and language about order and validity and the insistence upon the historic episcopate. The two traditions puzzle one another. The one seems legalistic; the other seems individualistic. To the one "intercommunion" is meaningless without unity of outward order; to the other "intercommunion" seems the one sensible and Christian way towards unity. And thus the debates between the two traditions are often wearisome and fruitless.

A fresh line of approach seems needed. Those who cherish the Catholic church and its historic order need to expound its meaning not in legalistic and institutionalist language, but in evangelical language as the expression of the gospel of God. In these pages church order, with its episcopate, creeds, and liturgy, will be studied in terms of the gospel. It will be asked what truth about the gospel of God does the episcopate, by its place in the one Body, declare? And what truth about the gospel is obscured if the episcopate is lacking or is perverted? If the historic structure of the church sets forth the gospel, it has indeed a meaning which the Evangelical Christian will understand, and it may be possible to show that reunion without that structure will impair that very gospel which the Evangelical Christian cherishes.

The philanthropists, outside or inside the Christian church, are also confronted with the death of the Messiah. They long passionately for the mitigation of the economic sufferings of humankind and for an effective international spirit. Their longing is after the obedience of Christ, for they know that Christ healed the sick and the possessed, and fed the bodies of men and women, and they look to the church to do the same. But as Jesus in the midst of his works of healing and feeding was moving towards death, so also is his church. For the church exists for something deeper than philanthropy and reform, namely to teach men and women to die to self and to trust in a resurrection to a new life which, because it spans both this world and another world, can never be wholly understood here and must always puzzle this world's idealists. Hence, as the Body of Christ crucified and risen, the church points men and women to a unity and a peace which they generally neither understand nor desire.

Thus the church is pointing beyond theology, beyond reunion-schemes, beyond philanthropies, to the death of the Messiah. It leads the theologian, the church-statesman, the philanthropist, and itself, also, to the cross. The dying is a stern reality; theologian, reunionist, philanthropist learn that their work and their idea is, in itself and of itself, nothing. But all that is lost is found; and the cross is the place where the theology of the church has its meaning, where the unity of the church is a deep and present reality, and where the church is already showing the peace of God and the bread from heaven to the nations. The Jews stumbled at the death and resurrection, and hence they never knew the church to be the Body of the Christ. The disciples knew it, only when he had died and was risen from the dead.

✌ 7 ‿

A Crisis of Faith

From *Canterbury Pilgrim*, pp. 4-7.

The storm over *Honest to God* broke in March 1963. I was at the time, after eighteen strenuous months in finding my feet in a new office [as Archbishop of Canterbury], scarcely prepared for a theological crisis. The initial error in reaction, in which I myself shared, was to think that the trouble was only that the author of the book was missing some of the profundities of the Christian faith and was being unnecessarily negative in expression. I think that was true. But I was soon to grasp how many were the contemporary gropings and quests which lay behind *Honest to God.*

I rather supposed that the need was to reaffirm the coherence of the faith on familiar lines, albeit with greater sensitivity and persuasion. If that was my initial mistake, I saw after a little further reflection that there was in the background a widespread crisis of faith which cried out for another kind of spirit in meeting it. I thus described this spirit, and if my words sounded at all new in the

contemporary Anglican scene they were in line with not a few of
the Anglican teachers of the past:

> Since the war our church has been too inclined to be concerned
> with the organising of its own life, perhaps assuming too easily
> that the faith may be taken for granted and needs only to be
> stated and commended. But we state and commend the faith
> only in so far as we go out and put ourselves with loving
> sympathy inside the doubts of the doubting, the questions of
> the questioners, and the loneliness of those who have lost their
> way. [2]

What had been happening? English theology has often been
very insular and unaware of trends on the continent of Europe.
The bomb which exploded in 1963 therefore caused the more
consternation in that it included, condensed within a single packet,
the quintessence of three divines as un-English as they were
different from one another: Tillich, Bonhoeffer, and Bultmann.
Tillich's substitution of the language of "ground of being" for the
familiar imagery of theism, Bonhoeffer's thesis of "Christianity
without religion," Bultmann's view that the gospel is an existen-
tialist encounter with Jesus without the framework of earth and
heaven and without the pattern of his historical career—all these
themes appeared in one package. These revolutions might perhaps
have been digested one at a time with the dilution and the finesse
with which English minds can sometimes absorb new and foreign
conceptions. But, coming all of a sudden and coming all together
within the covers of a single paperback, Tillich, Bultmann, and
Bonhoeffer made an explosion which could be heard.

The explosion, however, while it distressed many of the faithful
for whom we must care, was not unrelated to gropings, conscious
and unconscious, which had been widespread among many people
on the periphery of faith. There were those to whom the imagery
of God on a throne in heaven (imagery which they may never have
heard paraphrased intelligently) was wearisome, while they
warmed to the idea that something deep within themselves had
transcendent significance. There were those who had learned from

---

2. *Image Old and New* (London, 1963), p. 14.

Jesus that God is the God of the marketplace as well as the temple, and had wondered whether the God of "churchy" people was the same God. There were those who understood the meaning of an existential encounter with Jesus (though they would never use that language) and—however wrongly—felt encumbered by what seemed to be the load of myth and miracle. In fact a world of half-belief and half-doubt, of searchings and questionings, was being dug up by *Honest to God.* What was the orthodox teacher to do? He or she could show, I think with some truth, that in the Robinson thesis negative inferences seemed to be unduly emphasized and that orthodoxy was sometimes caricatured. But here was the opportunity to learn from that wistful world which was being uncovered, to understand, to discriminate, and then to try to guide with patience.

It soon was clear that *Honest to God* was only an item in a larger scene. There were other books and other excitements which illustrated the crisis of faith. I do not discuss here the "death of God" concepts.... But I mention a sad aspect of the malaise of faith: it coincided with a malaise concerning prayer and worship. It has been held to be one of the characteristics of Anglicanism that the tradition of prayer and worship intermingles with the work of theology, preaching, and practical service. The *lex orandi* has for us been felt to underlie the *lex credendi.* So it has sometimes happened that in times of intellectual disturbance, criticism, and change, when negatives tend to be prominent, the tradition of prayer and worship has kept alive the sense of Creator and creature, Savior and sinner, as the heart of what is essentially Christian. The sadness of the sixties was that the shocks of faith were synchronized with the querying of the practice of the spiritual life.

The querying of spirituality had its remoter and its nearer causes. There had been the long trend towards social activism in the Christianity of the West, and the reaction against "pietism." There was the growing urge to find transcendence through the world rather than away from it. Already present on the scene, the "non-prayer" tendency was heightened by the specific notions of secular Christianity as epitomized, for instance, in Harvey Cox's *The Secular City.* And among those who valued prayer there were some inhibiting ideas, like the idea that a "going apart" is to be deprecated as escapism—which meant being wiser than our Lord, who was found by Simon Peter praying alone in a desert place a great while before day.

These were some of the ingredients in the crisis of faith which loomed so large in the sixties. Faced by all this, there were many in the Church of England who found themselves burdened and embarrassed. A tendency came for theology to be polarized between those who were influenced by the new ideas and those who turned to an authoritarian and conservative biblical theology offering a security of faith which could sometimes include elements of fear and a failure to face the questionings of the mind. It was a test for "leadership." There were those who exhorted the faithful to be true to the gospel, lamented that these troubles had made the task of the Christian preacher difficult, and said in effect, "please do not rock the boat." There were those—and would that there had been more of them—who tried to combine a hold upon the deep values of tradition with a sensitive understanding of the turmoil. Questions needed to be faced, and need to be faced still. How far is a lifeless and undynamic use of religious imagery responsible for a misunderstanding of theism? How far does a tendency to exalt Jesus while professing to reject theism call for a deeper grasp of the Christlikeness of God among his exponents? May the negative concept of a religionless Christianity be redeemed into the positive theme of a lay spirituality?

These are real questions, and they are with us still. The lessons of the crisis of faith may have helped us and may help us still to know the glory of the Triune God, the creator, the judge, and the savior of human beings, and to proclaim it with more humility, more love, and more understanding of those who find faith hard. *O passi graviora*, it is through the facing of dark nights, whether in the mystery of God or in the agonies of the world, that the deepening of faith is realized.

ᴠ **8** ᴠ

Humanism and Contemporary Secularism

From *Sacred and Secular,* pp. 66-71.

Humanism is the doctrine that reverence for humanity and an understanding of human capacities are a sufficient clue to the fulfillment of human existence. Its view of humanity can be far from superficial; it sees human beings not only as eating and breeding and organizing their welfare but also as thinking and creating and devoting themselves to noble ends.

The Christian critique of humanism is clear enough. Humanism has neither the height nor the depth of the Christian doctrine of humanity. It knows neither the depth of men's and women's impotence and frustration as sinners, nor the height of their potentiality in the holiness which will lead to the vision of God in eternity. But if humanism is doing and saying things which on its own grounds are even fractionally good and true, the Christian critique must be accompanied by the most reverent understanding of what humanism is about.

Can we describe the issue thus? Humanism is a beautiful picture of some aspects of humanity. Round the picture, however, is a solid frame, and on the frame the words are inscribed "And that is all." Christians have to say that the frame is untrue. Furthermore, they have to say that the frame can, by its size and ugliness, cast shadows on the picture and blight its beauty. But nonetheless the picture contains what is true and beautiful and this fact can bring Christian and humanist near together. The Christian notices not only when humanism is the enemy, but also when it is within limits an ally. If Christians have as their thesis "Christians cannot be humanists," the sad response is encouraged, "humanists cannot be Christians."

The term "Christian humanism" has a long and honorable history; and its significance has changed in different phases. In its original form it meant the confluence of the Hebraic-Christian belief in the transcendent God, the creator and savior of human beings in their frailty, with the Greco-Roman belief in human beings in their beauty and dignity. Christian humanism in this classic sense flowered in the School of Alexandria, and Clement was its great exponent. The Christian humanism of Alexandria was, however, for the learned and the schools, and its product was the Christian Gnostic. As, however, the Christian faith, leavening the Latin races in the days of their victorious expansion, created the medieval civilization of the West, Christian humanism took on a wider and more diffused existence. There was a genuine synthesis of the religion of another world, of purgatory, hell, and heaven, with art, culture, and the common life. In different ways the *Divina Comedia* of Dante and the *Summa Theologica* of Thomas Aquinas witness to this synthesis. But it broke down. And it may not be too great a simplification of history to say that it broke down because it came to emphasize the supernatural in such a manner as to do less than justice to the natural. It saw human beings too exclusively in religious terms as candidates for heaven through the church's good offices from cradle to grave, and beyond the grave in purgatory, so that it devalued men and women in their own dignity with their reason and their conscience. It saw human sciences so subordinate to theology as their queen that their autonomy as sciences was not properly honored.

The Renaissance was the next upsurging of humanism, and Christian humanism had supreme opportunity. Its scope and potentialities were now vaster than ever before. Its role was not only, like Erasmus, to link Christian faith with the revival of classical letters, but also, like the Royal Society in England, to link Christian faith with the new scientific studies of nature....The study of nature, wherever it might lead, was one with the knowledge of God who is nature's author and sustainer.

The breakdown in its turn of the Christian humanism of the Renaissance is a complicated story. It includes the contrast and clash between Renaissance and Reformation, between the sense of the spiritual in human progress and the Reformation faith that human beings are depraved sinners justified by faith alone. This faith is indeed of the very heart of Christianity, and there can never be Christian renewal without it, but the recurring problem is its relation to "the light that lighteth every man." But beyond the tensions of Renaissance and Reformation the Christian humanism in the centuries which followed came to be strained by errors on both sides. On the one hand, there has been too much of a narrowly biblical theology and religion, literalistic and obscurantist, which denies the working of the divine *Logos* in the world's sciences. On the other hand, there have been within the realm of science tendencies to make particular aspects of one or two sciences do duty far beyond their proper power. Hence the clashes between "religion" and "science." Too often these have been clashes between a religion which distorts its own true character and a scientific theory negligent of science's own manysidedness.

So it is that Christian humanism has, after the scientific revolutions of the sixteenth, the nineteenth, and now the twentieth centuries, a task and a strain upon its own existence infinitely greater than in the earlier epochs. The lessons of its own history are deeply relevant for us, but the situations to which the lessons have now to be applied are alarmingly new. To the older cleavages between religion and humanism there has been added the hardening of much humanism into self-sufficient secularism. To the older sciences, never easily married with religion, there have been added new sciences which claim to understand human beings and manipulate their existence.[3] It may therefore be a very long time before Christian humanism will present itself again as an all-embracing synthesis. But it can meanwhile show itself in the lives of men and women, lives which are otherworldly and at the same time ready to throw themselves into the world's activities and to find God there. Such lives will be lives of faith, and such is the business of Christianity.

Sacred and secular, otherworldly and this-worldly, my conclusion is that Christianity is uncompromisingly both, both not in any facile Anglican or archiepiscopal compromise, but in a costly interrelation. We follow Christ who, in the form of a servant, made

---

3. In a note Bishop Ramsey refers to psychology, and he comments: "It should be the role of psychiatry not to be a substitute for moral decision but to enlarge the region of conscious moral decision. It is very misleading to equate psychological harmony with the goal of Christian holiness."

himself utterly one with humanity and history but was no less so, but rather drew the power to be so because he was found a great while before day alone in the desert place praying to the Father. As Christ was in the world and not of the world, so is his church called to be.

᠅ 9 ᔰ

Religion: Escape or Freedom?

A lecture given in October 1971 at Trinity College, Toronto; from *Canterbury Pilgrim*, pp. 55-64.

For centuries there have been those who have been anti-religion because they have been anti-God or anti-Christianity. In our own time, on the other hand, we have seen the new phenomenon of those who have been against religion in the name of God and of Christianity. There was Karl Barth's vigorous distinction between faith as an act which accepts God's gift by grace alone and religion as the human attempt to climb to God by pietistic exercises. There was Dietrich Bonhoeffer's thesis that religion belongs to human immaturity and that men and women are now called to stand on their own feet and find God in the courageous encounters of human life without the childish props of religious practice.... There is among very many young Christians in England, and I cannot doubt in Canada too, the insistence that no Christianity is credible which does not express itself urgently in practical service and in grappling with the issues of poverty and race. Is there not a widespread Christian activism impatient of religious practice?

Yet another wind is also blowing. In the last year or two specially I have felt its presence, for not infrequently when I am asked to address young people the request comes not for a talk about race or poverty or social action but for a talk about meditation or contemplation. There is the hunger for mysticism, the longing to escape from the pressures of environment so that the self may realize itself in freedom, in touch with a reality that transcends. At the one end there is the revived interest in the mystical techniques of Eastern religions, at the other end there is the use of drugs in the quest of ecstatic experience. Amid this mystical hunger Christianity is often written off, because its institutionalism inhibits spiritual adventure and because its activist preoccupations seem uninterested in religion. Here indeed is a judgment upon our Western Christendom if amid our eagerness to enhance the second great commandment we have failed to be true to our own mystical tradition and to help those whose hunger is a religious one....

How can a mere theologian be of service to those upon whom these two winds are blowing powerfully today? The theologian can try to see how they relate to the truth about God, humanity, and Christ. So let me make that attempt, not discouraged by Harvey Cox's remark, "You cannot expect jester's theology from the archbishop's palace."[4] Try we must, to see together in Christ the relation to God of which St. Irenaeus said, "The life of man is the vision of God," and the relation to the world of which the writer of the letter to Diognetus said, "As the soul is in the body, so are the Christians in the world."

Human beings exist to glorify their Creator. That is where we start. Glory and glorify are biblical words with very distinctive meaning. To glorify God is to reflect the radiance of God like a mirror, in a life of righteousness, justice, and compassion. But the nearer to God a person comes in so reflecting him, the more he or she is aware of his creaturely dependence, her unworthiness, his need for forgiveness, and the more she finds her joy in God himself in praise and gratitude. Those whom we call saints are people whose characters have been marked by the humility of the worshipping creature and the forgiven sinner. The goal of human beings created in God's image is heaven, for God in his love for them designs that their fellowship with himself will be perfected and will be unceasing. St. Augustine thus describes heaven:

> We shall rest and we shall see,
>   we shall see and we shall love,
> we shall love and we shall praise,
>   in the end which is no end.

---

4. *Feast of Fools,* p. 13.

Rest: we cease from our fussy busyness. *See,* because in thus resting our eyes will be opened and no longer blurred by our busyness, and we shall see God in his beauty and we shall see our fellows as they really are. Seeing, we shall not fail to *love:* to love our Creator and Savior and to love our fellows selflessly. But, resting, seeing, and loving, our joy will be in him who is the giver and the goal, in God himself, and so the last word will be *praise.* It will be an end which is no end: it will be finality, beyond which nothing is more perfect, but a perfection within which there will be endless new adventures in resting, seeing, loving, and praising.

Meanwhile human beings, with the hope of heaven in their hearts and with the hope of heaven giving the perspective of their present existence, are set to serve God within the world which God has created. With this world they are utterly involved, and their service of God is always through the world and not apart from it. In principle their relation to other people is the stuff and substance of their worship of God; but in their present imperfection they are compelled to see in a certain duality, albeit a duality like the two sides of a coin, their worship of God and their service of others.

Although we cannot expect jester's theology from an archbishop's palace, I recall some words of William Temple, who was indeed both a jester and a theologian:

> It is sometimes said that conduct is supremely important, and worship helps it. The truth is that worship is supremely important, and conduct tests it.

Isn't that right? The priority for human beings is their enjoyment of God for God's sake, in whom is the perfection of all that can be perfect; an enjoyment that can never be selfish as it is outgoing love responding to outgoing love; God can never be treated as if he were the means towards ends greater than himself. But because God is righteous there is no true worship of him that is not immediately reflected in the love and service of our neighbor in society. Our love and service of our neighbor, however, will be saved from being patronizing or possessive as in the doing of it we are humbled by God's forgiveness and by our knowing that God's glory is the goal of what we are trying to do.

It is on the ground of these main theological principles about God and us, the church and the world, that we need to see, to assess, to learn from, and if need be to correct the trends both of an activism which is often anti-religious and of neo-mysticism in its various forms....

Much of the anti-religious trend is, I believe, a reaction from misleading ideas about divine transcendence. God's transcendence does not mean that he is away from the world, living in some kind of space outside it. His beyondness is the beyondness of one who is here, everywhere, present in every human situation. It is here, everywhere, in every human situation that we know God, as one who is always here and always beyond here. Perhaps the older Christian spirituality tended too much to think of our serving God in the world in one direction, and then going off in another direction to find the God who transcends. We sometimes hear the phrase "new spirituality." I take it to mean that while God is indeed beyond we are to find his beyondness in and among life's daily circumstances. There will still be retreat, still withdrawal; but it will be a retreat and withdrawal from the surface of life so as to recollect the God who is the reality within it and beyond it.

Now for the other trend, "neo-mysticism."...Mysticism in the proper sense is an intense realization of God within the self and the self embraced within God in vivid nearness. It is a phenomenon known in a number of religions, and in those religions very similar language is used in describing the experience. There is deep darkness, the darkness of not knowing; and there is light with flashes in which the self knows the unknowable terribly near and knows itself as never before. Now through the centuries Christian teaching has emphasized that the significant thing is not just the mystic experience in itself but its place and its context within the whole life of a Christian. The experience is given by God sometimes to one who seeks God in a life of humility and charity, turned towards the righteousness as well as the beauty of God. And the effect of the experience of mystic union, sometimes described as "passive contemplation," is not to cause the person to long to have the experience again but to long to serve God and to do his will. Those who have had mystic experience will not want to tell everyone about it: they will have a longing to serve God in daily life, for in his *will* is our peace.

Mystic experience is given to some. But contemplation is for all Christians. Allow me a word about that prayer which is indeed for all of us. The prayer of Jesus our high priest is classically described in the sentence "he ever lives to make intercession for us." Now the Greek word which is here, and elsewhere, translated "intercede" does not mean to speak or to plead or to make requests or petitions: it means to *meet* someone, to *be with* someone in relation to or on behalf of others. Jesus is with the Father, for us. And our own prayer means essentially our being with God, putting ourselves in his presence, being hungry and thirsty for him, wanting him, letting heart and mind and will move towards him, with the needs of our world on our heart. It is a rhythmic movement of our personality into the eternity and peace of God and no less into the turmoil of the world for whose sake, as for ours, we are seeking God. If that is the heart of prayer, then the contemplative part of it will be large. And a church which starves itself and its members in the contemplative life deserves whatever spiritual leanness it may experience....

A prosperous religious culture with a deadened conscience about race or poverty is a monstrosity which brings its revenge. So too does an ethical and activist religion which starves itself by its neglect of contemplation....

St. Augustine said of old, *accedit verbum pani, et fit sacramentum:* Add together the Word and the Loaf, and the Sacrament is there. It is a sacrament which sustains us to be ourselves in Christ's body in the re-creation of the world. In the sacrament we are one with the risen Christ and we are united with the saints in heaven, with the Mother of our Lord and the holy angels; but as love is one and indivisible, the eucharist is the gate of heaven only as being also the gate through which we go out into the service of the world. So in this sacrament the neo-militants are given the humility with which alone their warfare will be Christian, the activists are called to silence for a space in the contemplation of a great mystery, the neo-mystics are shown that the one reality worth possessing is Christ crucified, and all of us are allowed to celebrate the sorrow and the joy of Christ.

III

WHAT MAKES
US ANGLICANS?

Bishop Ramsey was deeply committed to Christian unity, and he often met with leaders of other Christian communities. He always did so, however, as a committed Anglican. These selections demonstrate that he knew where he stood as an Anglican in the Christian community.

The first selection is from an early essay in which he defended and explained the uniqueness of Anglican theology against those who would deny that there was such a thing or who would try to reduce it to something else. Anglican theology, he believed, is rooted in its belief in the incarnation of God in Christ. From this belief derives its way of explicating the Christian faith. The sixteenth-century theologian Richard Hooker, he argues, was the first to develop an Anglican theology.

In one of his major works, *An Era in Anglican Theology,* he showed how Anglican theology made use of an incarnational methodology in dealing with the problems and controversies of a later time, the period between the First and Second World Wars. He was concerned to show both the weaknesses and strengths of such a theology, and he recognized that those were the weaknesses and strengths of Anglicanism itself.

As these writings demonstrate, Bishop Ramsey believed that the most significant contribution Anglicans could make to the universal church was to speak with a clear and knowledgeable voice about the Anglican tradition, as well as with an honest one. We should

not, he thought, try to hide our weaknesses, but neither should we
fail to appreciate our own heritage.

᜵ 10 ᔒ

What is Anglican Theology?

From "What is Anglican Theology?"
published in *Theology* (January, 1945), pp. 2-6.

There is such a thing as Anglican theology and it is sorely needed
at the present day. But because it is neither a system nor a
confession (the idea of an Anglican "confessionalism" suggests
something that never has been and never can be) but a method, a
use, and a direction, it cannot be defined or even perceived as a
"thing in itself," and it may elude the eyes of those who ask "What
is it?" and "Where is it?" It has been proved, and will be proved
again, by its fruits and its works.

The method, use, and direction characteristic of Anglican divinity first came into clear light in the writings of [Richard] Hooker.
His theology claimed to do both far less and far more than the
theologies of Calvin, of Luther, and of Trent. It did less in that it
eschewed any attempt to offer a complete scheme of biblical
doctrine, or an experiential assurance of justification, or an infalli-
bilist system of dogma. It did more in that it appealed to a larger
field of authority and dealt with the whole person rather than with
certain parts of him or her. For it appealed to scripture, tradition,
and reason: "the Spirit everywhere in the scripture...laboureth to
confirm us in the things which we believe by things whereof we
have sensible knowledge." And it dealt with the whole person, both
by its reverence for reason and conscience and by its refusal to draw
a circle around the inward personal element in religion and to
separate it from the world of external things. It was congruous with
all this that the incarnation, with the doctrine of the Two Natures,
was central, and that the church and the sacraments were closely
linked with the incarnation. The claim of this theology to be

"Catholic" rested not only upon its affinity with antiquity but upon the true "wholeness" of its authorities and of its treatment of human beings and their need. It offered them not only justification in their inward self but the sanctification of their whole being through sharing in the divine life....

The *bona fide* Anglican can never suffer the Latin scholastics to dominate the theology of his or her church. This refusal need not involve a depreciation of what the scholastics can do in the field of Christian philosophy. But the refusal must be made, because the scholastic would substitute other categories than those of the Bible at the very heart of theology, where the Anglican believes that only the biblical categories can rule. "I am not ashamed of the gospel, for therein is revealed a righteousness of God from faith unto faith": the appeal to scripture demands that God's revelation be understood first in these biblical categories, with the Greek of the New Testament as the theologian's primary apparatus. It is here that the quarrel really lies. This is not to deny that a far more humble and ready appreciation of the scholastic's work is needed among us; but this is to say that it can never be suffered to possess the central shrine.

Equally the *bona fide* Anglican is not at home with the divinity broadly and somewhat incorrectly called Barthian. It would be futile to belittle what has been learned and needs to be learned from the Barthian school concerning the failure of the "liberal" treatment of the Bible, the realities of God's transcendence, grace, and judgment, and the more truly theological perspective in biblical interpretation. Yet the Anglican's gratitude for this is no longer leaving him or her blind to the need for revolt and protest, akin to the revolt and protest of Hooker against the Calvinism of his day. A concentration upon the Word spoken which misses the importance of the Word made flesh, a concentration upon justification which as good as denies the theme of sanctification, a concentration upon certain elements in St. Paul which omits the teaching of St. John (particularly chapters 6 and 17) from its picture of Christianity, betoken a divinity which is less than truly biblical.

Nor can the Anglican fail to notice the loosening of the neo-Calvinists' hold upon the incarnation as a central principle. Partly this is seen in a failure to make that estimate of humankind which the incarnation demands. Partly this is seen in a readiness (observable in different degrees in some writers) to part with the idea of the incarnation itself, since if all that is needed is "an irruption into history for man's salvation" there is no special importance in the doctrine of God made Man....

There seems to lie before Anglican divinity the immense task which is also an immense opportunity: to appeal once again to the threefold authority of scripture, tradition, and reason: not to repeat in archaic fashion the appeal as it was made in the sixteenth century, but to discover its new mode as it is needed today.

As to scripture, the way is open for a treatment that avoids the errors and the violence of much modern work. The liberal method drew out the human nature of the Bible but misinterpreted it through losing its theological key. In reaction the "new school" has recovered a belief in the divine nature of the Bible but has often refused a due place to its human nature by ignoring questions of historicity, by trying to settle critical problems by theological affirmations, and by over-simplifying the rough, jagged process wherein the theology was hammered out in the history. Is there not need for a treatment of biblical questions, an exposition of biblical themes, an assessment of biblical authority which holds in view the Two Natures of the Bible? And is this not a task akin to that which Hooker performed in a different though cognate field?

But the interpreter of scripture cannot work without presuppositions, and the disciple of Hooker approaches the Bible with presuppositions learned from the living tradition of the church. But the appeal to tradition cannot mean today precisely what it meant in the sixteenth century or in the writings of the Tractarians. It needs rethinking. In place of a static appeal to the undivided church (for the Holy Ghost has said many things since the great schism) we should perhaps think in terms of the appeal to Christian experience. This appeal will put the utmost emphasis upon the inward experience of Christians and its moral fruits; but it will not, in the manner of Hooker's opponents, draw a closed circle around the inward aspect of the Christian life. It will instead include the form and the sacramental life of the church in their witness to the historical givenness of the gospel. Though the form without the Spirit is dead, it is through the Spirit's use of the form—in creed, sacrament, order, liturgy—that the Spirit preserves the true salt of Christian life in its union with the objectivity of gospel and church.

As to the appeal to reason, the writer of this paper would rather that others, with a philosophical equipment which he lacks, took up the tale. But perhaps the nature of the Anglican's appeal to reason may be discovered partly from the nature of the appeal to scripture and tradition, and partly from the distinction (deep in the Anglican's bones) between authority and infallibility. "Two things there are that trouble these latter times: one is that the church of Rome cannot, another that Geneva will not err." Where is the secret of a theology which does not require the infallible logician and yet "proves all things," as the apostle said, and speaks not to part of a person but to the whole of him or her, *justifying* and *sanctifying* and *illuminating* body, soul, and spirit whole and entire unto the coming of the Lord?

In these tasks Anglicans will not suppose that they have a system or a confession that can be defined and commended side by side with those of others; indeed, the use of the word "Anglicanism" can be very misleading. Rather will they claim that their tasks look beyond "isms" to the gospel of God and to the Catholic Church which they try to serve with a method, use, and direction needed as greatly today as in the past.

⋌ **11** ⋋

Characteristics of Anglican Theology

From *An Era in Anglican Theology*, pp. 164-170.

In the perspective of history we can see that this era [from Bishop Charles Gore to Archbishop William Temple] possessed many permanent characteristics of Anglican theology. Theological history resembles an iceberg in that there is a part of it which is below the surface, and it is the part which gives ballast and continuity. Among the half-conscious influences there is the influence which a prayer book inevitably has in a liturgical church. The *lex orandi* has its quiet and unobtrusive effect upon the *lex credendi*.

Throughout the story [of this era], certain factors of Anglican continuity have seldom been absent. First, the Platonist strain had been characteristic of Anglican divinity since the sixteenth century. Visitors from other theological traditions have often noticed it in us, and—what is significant—they have sometimes noticed our own unawareness of it. It has accounted for the tone of classical humanism in Anglican divinity, sometimes at the expense of the Hebraic aspect of our faith. It has kept at bay the Aristotelian scholastic spirit. Within this era it helped to set a limit to the influence of Hegelian idealism....The Platonist strain linked our era with the continuing story of Anglicanism. But there was the big difference between Inge, for whom Platonism was a primary medium for theology itself, and Gore and Temple, for whom it was a handmaid with—as between the two of them—somewhat different roles.

Second, there is the Anglican sensitivity to the significance of spirituality, the life of prayer, for theology. We see this often, from Lancelot Andrewes to William Temple. In the present century the growing interest in the study of religious experience, of the psychology of religion and of mystical phenomena seen in that context, might have led many into subjectivism and shallowness, had not Anglican thought drawn upon the deep stream of Christian spirituality coming from past centuries....

Then there is the constant Anglican devotion to scripture and the [church] fathers, and some of this appeared in our era with a detachment from the flux of current tendencies....

Finally, there is the constant Anglican care for the *via media*. This has been seen in different ways. It is seen in the choice of middle ground between strongly entrenched rival camps—like Hooker's middle ground between Rome and Geneva. It is seen in the dislike of pressing aspects of theology with the ruthless logic of a self-contained system. It is seen in the tendency for mediation between schools of thought or religious movements within, or without, our church. It is seen in the instinct for distinguishing doctrines of lesser and greater import, a bequest of Hooker to the ages which followed him. This care for *via media* was strongly present in divines of our era....

These influences made for integrity and for depth at a time when facile and shallow syntheses were all too easy. If these dangers were not avoided, they were at least corrected by influences deeper than contemporary fashions....

One day the history of Anglican theology from 1939 to 1959 will be written. We can here do no more than note briefly and broadly what has been happening, and ask, *Quo tendimus?*

There has been a big change in the relation of theology to the world around it and in the nature of theology as its exponents see it. In place of a common stock of friendly philosophical tendencies for theology to exploit and a body of accepted ethical concepts to which theology could be relevant, there is now a lack of unity both in intellectual concepts and in moral standards. There is the intensely technological culture, to which the language of religion means little. In such an environment the isolation of biblical theology is very plain. The work of the theologian is understood as the exposition of the Bible "from within." If it be indeed true that the gospel is less muffled by attempts at synthesis with the culture of an age, it is no less true that its contact with the age is sometimes far to seek.

Within the world of theology, however, the isolation of Anglicanism has grown less. Prophetic teachers from Europe and America drew English minds beyond the writers of their own church and country. The ecumenical spirit aroused the interest of different confessions in one another. Anglicans found themselves more involved in general theological trends. There was the new valuation of Old Testament theology in relation to the Hebrew cultus. There were the new interests within New Testament study: the gospels as "theological documents," typology, theological word-study. There was the revival of study of the fathers. There was the revival of liturgical study, not least in unexpected regions. There was a new attention to religious language, partly on account of a concern about "communication," and partly on account of the questions raised by modern linguistic philosophy. None of these energies is uniquely Anglican. In all of them Anglicans have borne a worthy part by their scholarly work.

Within the Anglican Communion a reshaping of schools of thought and parties has been in process. Anglo-Catholicism is a less consciously defined body, and its ideals and methods are more diffused. Liberal Modernism has waned. Conservative Evangelicalism had a revival, partly aided by the craving for authoritarian security in the tempestuous post-war years. Unity has increased by a greater understanding of the oneness of word and sacrament in the liturgy, and the sense of the church with the altar of God as its center has deepened. So, too, has the conviction of the mission of the laity within the church.

There is, however, a distinctive witness still to be borne by Anglican theology out of the depths of its own tradition. Biblical theology is in an unsatisfactory state. It cannot be naively invoked as the solution for everything. There is here a task that Anglican theology can yet perform, by keeping alive the importance of history in the manner of its great divines of the past, by strenuous attempts to relate biblical revelation to other categories of thought in the contemporary world, by striving to integrate dogma with spirituality in the life of prayer, by presenting the church as the effectual sign of the supernatural in the midst of the natural order. No less is it necessary to avoid imbibing uncritically the assumptions of contemporary ecumenism, and to meet them with something deeper, if less immediately popular, drawn from our appeal to scripture and antiquity.

In these tasks not a little can be learned from this era [from Bishop Gore to Archbishop William Temple]. Our eyes can be helped to distinguish synthesis which is superficial and synthesis which is surely grounded, arbitrary liberalism and genuine liberality, facile comprehensiveness and true theological coherence. The fifty years of our study have much to show as to how theology can, and cannot, ally itself to the culture of an age.

There has been in recent years much striving after order and tidiness. But the theological coherence which a Gore or a Temple exhibited came, not from a quest of tidiness, but from a vigorous wrestling with truth for truth's sake. Without such theological coherence, the church's moral witness may appear as piecemeal bits of moralizing, and the majestic unity of the church's faith may be too faintly made visible.

⌇ **12** ⌇

The Incarnation

From *An Era in Anglican Theology*, pp. 27-29.

Modern Anglican theology owes many of its characteristics to the central place held within it by the incarnation. Anglicanism has, for instance dwelt much on the Nicene and Chalcedonian dogmas and on those ancient fathers who directly interpreted them. Always somewhat insular in its attitude to continental theology, Anglicanism in these years [from 1889 to 1939] paid little heed to continental movements and writers, except when they concerned the Person of Christ, in history or dogma: as did the writings of Harnack, Ritschl, and Schweitzer. Furthermore, the doctrine of the Incarnate Christ as the *Logos* gave a constant impulse towards relating the incarnation, wherever possible, with contemporary movements in thought or social progress.

The question is now being asked in retrospect: is there an inevitable loss in theological perspective or proportion if the incarnation is allowed to become the center of theology?

It must once more be insisted that the theology of Gore and his disciples was emphatically a theology of redemption. The incarnation was effectual only because the Incarnate died and rose again, and the very mode and manner of the incarnation were determined by its redemptive character. Nonetheless, when the incarnation is made the center it easily follows that: *explanation* rather than *atonement* can tend to dominate the theological scene, and *reason* can depress the place and meaning of *faith* in the approach to revealed truth. The giving of prominence to this particular dogma can also cause other categories of biblical language and thought to recede from their rightful prominence. These weaknesses have been alleged in the long-term effects of the Anglican incarnational theology.

There is some truth in the allegations. First, with the incarnation as its center, theology can cause its adherents to cherish it as a means of explaining the world, as if to say: "Thanks to the incarnation, nature and man make sense, and the world has unity and meaning." That is indeed a proper role for theology to have. But it proved possible for philosophical theologians so to pursue it as to travel far from the sort of faith which, seeing no hope for a world sin-racked and frustrated, throws itself empty on the cross of Christ and knows that the world *cannot* be explained until it has been radically changed....

Again, with the incarnation as its center, the concept of revelation easily becomes somewhat intellectualized by a sort of rationalism. Such rationalism may appear in a tendency to speak as if we moved progressively from discerning God in nature to discerning him in humanity, and thence to discerning him in Christ—whereas it may be that it is only through knowing God in Christ that we are able to believe in him in relation to nature and humanity.

Third, may not the use of the incarnation as the central principle go hand-in-hand with a soft-pedalling of other biblical categories? There have been occasions when the Anglican divinity of our period assumed the incarnation as the basis, and thence passed on to various nonbiblical categories for its exposition. This is a process amply justified in the work of interpretation. But there is the danger that while the Bible serves as the ground and base of theology it is not quite allowed to tell its own tale in its own way. The Bible contains theological themes which "incarnation" alone does not convey.

These *gravamina,* therefore, have cause. But they are rightly seen only alongside what the Anglican theology of incarnation was achieving. It enabled a genuine contact between supernatural religion and contemporary culture. It enabled a meeting-place between revelation and the keen contemporary sense of the importance of historical inquiry. In the hands of such an exponent as Charles Gore, it was impregnated with the conviction that Christ is known only as the restorer of a sinful race, and that divine truth is known only by those who will stand under the divine judgment. Furthermore, it enabled modern Anglicanism to face many modern tasks with its roots still in the fathers of the ancient church; and it conserved in modern Anglicanism that sense of the creature's adoration of the Creator which the doctrine of the Word-made-flesh keeps ever at the heart of religion.

⤳ **13** ⤳

Liberal Catholicism

"Liberal Catholicism and Essays Catholic and Critical," from *An Era in Anglican Theology*, pp. 100-110.

Based upon the authority of scripture interpreted by tradition, the Catholic faith, [Charles] Gore insists, commends itself by its own rational coherence and by its congruity with the known facts about the world which science and moral experience have discovered. If the Catholic faith has its own inner coherence, so too has the modernist version of Christianity; given its assumptions, its elements cohere together, but its assumptions do not agree with the experience of humanity in its need of supernatural salvation. As he was wont, Gore asked his readers to test his case by reason at every point.

Gore called the presentation of the faith which he favored "Liberal Catholicism." It was a favorite phrase. By "Catholicism" he meant

> that way of regarding Christianity which would see in it not merely or primarily a doctrine of salvation to be apprehended by individuals, but the establishment of a visible society as the one divinely constituted home of the great salvation, held together not only by the inward Spirit but also by certain manifest and external institutions.[1]

By this he meant that the belief in the Catholic Church must go hand-in-hand with the constant appeal to scripture as the standard of doctrine and moral judgment (the two are inseparable in impor-

---

1. *Catholicism and Roman Catholicism*, p. 1.

tance) and the constant concern for the intellectual integrity of the individual. "Liberal Catholicism" was, Gore believed, precisely embodied in the Anglican appeal to scripture, antiquity, and reason. The favorite term did not mean for Gore a party, or a type of religion, or a particular set of tenets. It was for him virtually synonymous with Anglicanism as rightly understood, for the Church of England in its inherent character appeals to scripture and tradition and reason, and thus bears witness to the Holy Catholic Church of Christ in a way in which Rome (through its errors) cannot, and the East (through its intellectual conservatism) does not. It was a witness all too often obscured by compromises, and tremendous in its moral demands, yet embodied in the Anglican vocation from the first....

Liberal Catholicism found its days numbered with the coming of the Second World War. The movements towards dogma and scholasticism, towards the transcendental theology of the Word in the Bible, and away from the spirit of synthesis with the contemporary age, came in full flood. The categories of experience and piety, of evolution and apologetics, gave place to the categories of theology in its classic forms. The gulf seemed great: the denigrations across it were plentiful. But the questions asked by Liberal Catholicism have a way of returning, and are not to be pushed aside. Both the earlier and the later phases of Liberal Catholicism had their faults. If the faults of the later phase ought not to blind us to the importance of its quest, the faults of the earlier ought not to blind us to its perception of the coherence of the Christian faith.

IV

THE GLORY OF GOD

Here is Michael Ramsey as a biblical scholar and theologian. As all of his writings make clear, the Bible was the source for his spirituality and for his intellectual presentations of Christian belief. He would return to it over and over again in order to draw from it the deep things which he believed the church and the world need to hear.

These selections from *The Glory of God and the Transfiguration of Christ* are fairly technical, and they deserve careful attention. They show what a wise scholar, who is also attuned to pastoral needs, can do with biblical material. If today many preachers avoid dealing with scripture because it seems to them to be "foreign" to the modern world, Ramsey provides a forceful alternative. The study of a word, such as "glory," can open up the scriptures. It can show how the biblical account of God's dealing with human beings is unified and exciting.

"Glory" was a principal theme in Ramsey's own writings. For him it drew together both the despair and the hope of humankind: our alienation and separation from God and yet our hope in God through Christ. The idea of "glory" was thus closely linked with the incarnation of God in Christ. In Jesus Christ we can see how we are reconciled to God and, thus, how our humanity is called into the glory of God. Michael Ramsey the theologian and pastor always insisted that the last word about the human condition is the word of hope in Christ, who is both the glory of our humanity and the manifestation of the glory of God.

∿ **14** ∿

Basic Convictions

From *Introducing the Christian Faith*, pp. 8-9.

Anyone who sets out to present the Christian faith today is up against the problem of religious language. It is not only that the distinctive Christian vocabulary is remote from much contemporary culture, but also that the types of proposition and thought-form are remote as well. My own reaction to the problem is this. There needs to be a greater acknowledgment of the poetical character of much religious language, with more frank explanation that this is so. There is the need to avoid such theological technicalities as are avoidable or capable of genuine paraphrase. There is the need to try to show that much about which the Christian faith speaks is happening within the experience of ordinary people, and that the Christian language focuses and interprets what is theirs already rather than assaults them with some sort of hobby or technicality from without. But there is also the need for those unavoidable Christian words with whose meaning anyone asking about the Christian faith much grapple, whether it be a word like "sin," untranslatable because of its ugly incisiveness, or a word like "glory," untranslatable because of the wealth of ideas which it contains for the imagination.

～ **15** ～

The Glory of Yahveh
From *The Glory of God and the Transfiguration of Christ*, pp. 9-22.

The word "glory" in the English versions of the Old Testament is a translation of the Hebrew word *kabod*. Coming from a root which denotes "heaviness" or "weight," the word often means the "riches" or the "distinction" of a person or nation. Thus Laban's sons complain, "Jacob hath taken away all that was our father's; and of that which was our father's hath he gotten all the glory" (Gen. 31:1). And the psalmist gives the warning: "Be not thou afraid when one is made rich, when the glory of his house is increased: for when he dieth he shall carry nothing away; His glory shall not descend after him" (Ps. 49:16-17). The *kabod* of a nation is its prosperity (cf. Isa. 16:14, 17:4, 21:16, 61:6); and, more than that, it is the distinction amid the world of nations which its prosperity expresses.

A more personal use of the word also appears. *Kabod* can mean a person's self or spirit. The inward spirit of a person is that person's glory, the thing wherein the person's weight or worth is believed to consist. Sometimes the word is thus used with an intensity of feeling: "Therefore my heart is glad, and my glory rejoiceth" (Ps. 16:9); "My heart is fixed, O God; I will sing, yea, I will sing even with my glory" (Ps. 108:1). Jacob, denouncing the violence of his sons Simeon and Levi, cries: "O my soul, come not into their council; unto their assembly, my glory, be not thou united" (Gen. 49:6). Perhaps the spirit is, in poetic speech, the glory of a person because it is the noblest part.

It is this word that is used to express the great theological conception [of] the glory of God. If the conception is rich and complex in its final development this is no less true of its early history. *Kabod* denotes the revealed being or character of Yahveh, and also a physical phenomenon whereby Yahveh's presence is made known; and scholars have not been agreed as to the priority in time of one or other of these uses....

If the problem of origins has not been wholly solved, we are not prevented from examining the content of the biblical teaching.

There can be no question that the presence of Yahveh was often connected with a storm of thunder and lightning. The imagery of thunder, lightning, fire, cloud, darkness recurs both in theophanies and in metaphorical descriptions of Yahveh's intervention in human affairs. The influence of the imagery seems to be far-reaching. The thunder is Yahveh's voice, the lightning is his arrows and spear; and it has been suggested that the cherubim and seraphim are creatures derived from the serpent-like lightning. We see the conception in the darkness, fire, and smoke of Sinai, where volcanic imagery may also play its part. We see it also in the song of Deborah and Barak, who tell of how the intervention of Yahveh in a storm brought victory to Israel. We see it above all in the brilliant storm-theophany of Psalm 18. And in the storm-picture in Psalm 29 the word *kabod* significantly occurs....

Important however as is the storm-theophany, there are traces of another conception of the *kabod* in a pre-exilic stratum of the Pentateuch. In Exodus 33:12-23, the "J writer" seems to be writing of a theophany of Yahveh in human form. First, Moses is told: "My presence will go with thee, and I will give thee rest." Then, Moses is bold to ask: "Show me, I pray thee, thy glory," and the answer comes that Moses must stand in a cleft of the rock while Yahveh passes by, and will then see only the back of Yahveh. Perhaps the word *kabod* is here used to mitigate the anthropomorphism of the story. It seems that the importance of the passage lies in its suggestion that in pre-exilic times the storm-theophany was not the *only* known idea of the glory of Yahveh.

Sooner or later, however, the *kabod* appears in the Old Testament literature with the meaning of the character of Yahveh as revealed by his acts in history. There are a few passages in the Pentateuch where the *kabod* seems to suggest not the phenomena which indicate the presence of Yahveh so much as the *character* of Yahveh, made known to Israel by his mighty works as her deliverer and guide (Num. 14:22; Deut. 5:24). Here we touch the distinctive note of Israel's faith—the faith that Yahveh is not only a God who may be found in this or that locality or meteorological phenomenon, but also a God who has intervened in history to deliver Israel, made a covenant with her, and revealed to her his stern moral demands and his righteous purpose. It is a faith that does not necessarily discard "meteorology," but blends the meteorological and the ethical in its conception of God, as some of the psalms were to show (cf. Ps. 97:2-6).

It is above all in the prophets that this theology of the *kabod* confronts us. Perhaps Isaiah of Jerusalem had a decisive influence upon it, as a result of his record of the vision which he saw in the temple (Isa. 6:1-4). It is unlikely that this language can be dissociated from a quasi-physical conception. But the prophet's mind is at work on other levels than this. The glory of Yahveh is linked with his holiness; and if the holiness means a remoteness from all that is unrighteous, the glory is that union of sovereignty and righteousness which is the essence of the divine character.

> This holy, moral power, which is revealed to Isaiah in his vision, is the Lord of the heavenly hosts, and the whole world reflects the lustre of his righteousness. History, human life is under the government of a righteous power that rules the world, and is not devoted merely to satisfying the unethical desires of a petty nation or tolerating its sins.[1]

Isaiah's words have a significance for the revelation of the glory of God that reaches far beyond the Old Testament into the worship of the Christian church. In the liturgy of the church the adoration of the divine glory in the words of the song of the seraphim immediately precedes the eucharistic action in which the glory of the cross of Christ is set forth.

The second Isaiah, the prophet of the exile, went further than his predecessor. He made explicit the monotheism which the first Isaiah implied, and proclaimed a God who is incomparable, the Lord of history, the only God, the first and the last, the potential Savior of all the nations. Writing on the eve of the great deliverance that enabled the exiles to return to Jerusalem, he sees this deliverance as a drama in which the glory of Yahveh is disclosed (Isa.

---

1. G. B. Gray, *Isaiah*, International Critical Commentary, pp. 106-107.

40:4-5). Yahveh will not "give his glory to another" (42:8, 48:11), and his people are those who are "called by my name, and whom I have created for my glory" (43:7).

Finally, the post-exilic writer of Isaiah 60 pictures Jerusalem as the scene of the shining-forth of the glory of Yahveh to the nations (Isa. 60:1-3). Here the idea of radiance has the greatest prominence. Indeed, in the *kabod* of Yahveh radiance, power, and righteous character are inextricably blended; and the word thus tells of a theology in which the attributes of God in himself are inseparable from his attractiveness and saving activity in the world. Israel's knowledge of God's glory has its corollary in Israel's obligation to reflect God's character. If, for instance, she cares for the poor and the naked, she has the promise:

> Then shall thy light break forth as the morning, and thy healing shall go forth speedily; and thy righteousness shall go before thee; the glory of the Lord shall be thy rearward. (Isa. 58:8)

The psalmists tell a similar tale. But to a greater extent they use the word in connection with the *future* manifestation of the glory and the recognition of the glory by the nations. Yahveh is the "king of glory" (Ps. 24:7-10), and the acknowledgment of this in all the world will be the consummation of his purpose (Pss. 96:3, 57:11, 85:9-10). Thus the psalmists unite with the prophets in using the word glory to tell of Yahveh's universal sovereignty and its future vindication.

When all this has been said only the half has been told about the doctrine of the *kabod,* for there is also the special conception that appears in the exilic and post-exilic writings of the Priestly School. Here the *kabod* is connected with a local theophany on Mount Sinai or in the tabernacle and the temple. It is a physical phenomenon, manifest to ordinary vision. At the same time, it has to be remembered that this "localized" conception is held in tension with a deepened conviction that Yahveh is transcendent and never to be confined to any earthly dwelling.

In the fashioning of this conception it seems that Ezekiel, the prophet of the earlier years of the Babylonian exile, had a big influence. Though he is familiar with the idea of the *kabod* as the divine character (cf. Ezek. 39:21), he uses the word almost always of a fiery appearance descried in his own visions. It is bright as a rainbow (1:28, 10:4), it moves (9:3, 10:4, 43:2), it is borne upon cherubim (10:19, 11:22), it is accompanied by the sound of a great rushing (3:12). In his opening vision by the banks of the river Chebar, Ezekiel, amid the dazzling phenomena of the storm-cloud, the four living creatures, the chariot, and the appearance of a man, saw the fiery brightness which was "the appearance of the likeness of the glory of the Lord." And he fell upon his face, awestruck at the transcendent and omnipresent God who makes his presence known to exiles in Babylonia no less than to the people in Jerusalem....

The Priestly Writer [in his narratives of the wilderness, of Sinai, and the tabernacle] tells of the Mosaic period in the wilderness so as to make his narrative reflect the belief and institutions of himself and his school in the post-exilic period. But he builds upon earlier traditions.... The Priestly Writer has his own conception. The cloud appears at Sinai. It is seen in the camp only when the tabernacle has been completed. It dwells continually in the tabernacle. By day it is seen as a cloud, by night as a fiery pillar. If it should be seen to be fiery by day, there unmistakably is the *kabod.* The cloud is not itself the glory, nor is it part of a set of storm-phenomena which constitute the glory. Rather, it is a covering which conceals the glory that shines through it from within. At Sinai the first appearance took place. Moses entered the cloud and went up onto the mount, and there remained forty day and forty nights. And when he descended the skin of his face shone and he put a veil over it to conceal it from the people when he spoke with them (Exod. 24:16-17, 34:29-35)....

It is significant that the post-exilic literature, while it dwells upon the presence of the glory in the ancient tabernacle, nowhere speaks of the glory as present in the *contemporary* post-exilic temple. The priestly theology lacked a note of confidence. The longings of Israel were not satisfied. The fulfillment of the exilic prophecies had not been completed; and these prophecies became more and more projected into the future. But the hope remains; and one day Israel will have the vision of the *kabod* of her God, whether by his dwelling with humans upon the stage of history or

by the coming of a new heaven and a new earth bathed in the light
of the divine radiance.

We pass now beyond the books of the Hebrew canon of the Old
Testament, and find two developments in late pre-Christian Judaism which are of great importance. The first is the conception of
shekinah. The growing sense of the divine transcendence caused
the Hebrew mind to shrink from references to the direct intervention of Yahveh in human affairs. Hence in the Targums, or rabbinic
paraphrases of scripture, certain Aramaic words were used as
"buffers" to enable the divine intervention to be described without
the language of direct description.... Of these words the *shekinah*
is the most prominent....

The *shekinah* is not the glory. Only once in the Targums is the
word used as a translation of *kabod* (Zech. 2:9); and in many
passages *shekinah* and glory are clearly distinguished, as when the
Targum of Leviticus 26:12 says: "I will place the glory of my
shekinah among you." Nor is the *shekinah* a personal or hypostatic
intermediary with attributes and functions. Rather, it is a way of
speaking about God such as conveys the truth of his omnipresence,
accessibility, and special activity within the created world without
infringing the doctrine of his transcendence....

The idea of the *shekinah* expresses the Jewish conception of
the divine in a way that easily eludes exact understanding on the
part of a non-Jew.

> The conception made God as near to every worshipper as any
> modern man could desire. To the first century is attributed the
> explanation why God revealed himself in the lonely thorn bush.
> It was to teach that no spot upon the earth is empty of *shekinah*.
> Yet it was finely perceived that God is in one sense only "near"
> when his creatures are present, and ready to apprehend his
> nearness. It is they who for practical purposes turn his transcen-
> dence into immanence. Hence the doctrine that virtue, Israel,
> the sanctuary and the Law, all bring down God or the *shekinah*
> from heaven to earth, while sin and idolatry remove him. Yet
> the divine nearness realized by the Israelite through the Law did
> not interfere with the theoretic apprehension that God was not,
> like a human person, limited by any particular place.[2]

The differences therefore between the rabbinic conception of the *shekinah* and the biblical conception of the *kabod* are as significant as the resemblances. These came to be fused in the language and doctrine of the Septuagint. The word *doxa* represented both *kabod* and *shekinah*; and the word *skene* represented both tabernacle and *shekinah*. Hence conceptions which are distinct in Hebrew and Aramaic literature became, in the Septuagint, fused into a unified imagery of God's glory and God's dwelling or tabernacling with his people. This unified imagery is the background of much of the thought of the writers of the New Testament.

The other late development is the imagery of the messianic glory, particularly in the apocalyptic books. Glory is an attribute of the Messiah, of the righteous in the messianic age and sometimes of heaven and earth themselves when they shall be drenched in the light of the divine radiance....

Such is the unity in diversity of the doctrine of the glory of God in Israel. There is a unity because from very early times the conception of the *kabod* was linked with Israel's faith in a righteous and sovereign God. There is a diversity because the faith of Israel did not drop in a neat pattern from heaven but was wrought out in the ups and downs of a turbulent history. Nowhere are the tensions of biblical theology greater than in the doctrine of the glory. It speaks on the one hand of an invisible and omnipresent God and on the other hand of a meteorological phenomenon; on the one hand of Israel's transcendent king and judge and on the other hand of a presence tabernacling in Israel's midst. But in these tensions the validity of the theology of the Old Testament lies. "Am I a God at hand, saith the Lord, and not a God afar off?" (Jer. 23:23). Always in tension these contrasted aspects of the divine glory find their true unity when the Word by whom all things were made became flesh and dwelt among us, and the glory of Bethlehem and Calvary is the glory of the eternal God.

---

2. C. G. Montefiore in *The Beginnings of Christianity*, vol. I, pp. 38-39.

⌁ **16** ⌁

Glory in the New Testament

From *The Glory of God and the Transfiguration of Christ*, pp. 27-28.

Within the theological use [of *doxa*] in the New Testament it is sometimes the idea of light and radiance that is prominent. Both in the sayings of Jesus about the future Parousia, and in the teaching of the apostles about the heavenly state of Jesus and the future destiny of the Christians, *doxa* describes a celestial brightness and splendor. Sometimes, on the other hand, the emphasis of the word is upon the character or power of God, and the phrase "the riches of his glory" (Eph. 1:18) is a reminder of the biblical roots of the doctrine. It seems that references to the rabbinic idea of the *shekinah* are, despite the indiscriminate language used by some modern writers, infrequent. The apostles pierce through the later Jewish developments to the *biblical* ideas of the glory, and find these ideas coming to rest in the revelation of God in Jesus Christ.

It is often hard to determine which aspect of the glory is present in a particular passage, and indeed the different aspects melt into one another in the New Testament as in the Old. But in every aspect of the glory the person of Jesus Christ becomes the dominant fact. Insofar as *doxa* means the power and character of God, the key to that power and character is found in what God has done in the events of the gospel. Insofar as *doxa* is the divine splendor, Jesus Christ *is* that splendor. And insofar as a state of light and radiance awaits the Christ as the final destiny, that light and radiance draw their meaning from the presence and person of Christ. Hence new possibilities of language emerge: such is the place of Jesus Christ in relation to the divine glory that it is possible to speak of *the glory of Christ*, and by those words to mean no less than the glory of God himself.

It follows that the word *doxa* both reflects and expresses the pattern of the apostolic faith. This faith has as its groundwork the glory of God in creation, in nature, and in the history of Israel; it has as its center the glory of God in the birth, life, death, and exaltation of Jesus, and as its goal the participation of humankind and of all creation in the eschatological glory of the Messiah. Creation, redemption, eschatology form a single pattern; and to separate them is to render each of them unintelligible and to distort the theology of the apostolic age.

⋌ **17** ⋎

Glory in St. Paul

From *The Glory of God and the Transfiguration of Christ*, pp. 46-56.

S t. Paul was a Hebrew of Hebrews, and nowhere is this more plain than in his thinking about the glory of God. While there are, at most, only a very few traces in his writings of the rabbinic doctrine of the *shekinah*, we find him alluding not seldom both to the scriptural doctrine of the *kabod* and to the apocalyptic hope of the messianic glory. To him the glory of God is the character and power of God, known in creation, in providence, and in history. If he does not say in so many words that "the heavens declare the glory of God" he certainly believes it, "for the invisible things of him since the creation of the world are clearly seen, being perceived through the things that are made, even his everlasting power and divinity" (Rom. 1:20). But humankind is unresponsive. Idolaters "changed the glory of the incorruptible God into the likeness of the image of corruptible man" (Rom. 1:23), and the whole race "fell short of the glory of God" (Rom. 3:23).[3] So the devout Pharisee

---

3. In a note Ramsey says that Paul is here alluding to the rabbinic idea that Adam was created with a ray of the divine glory on his face, and this ray was lost in the Fall and briefly restored at Sinai, only to be lost again. The rabbinic idea would suggest that the glorifying of human beings in the new creation is the realization of their true meaning.

looks forward to the messianic glory that is to be, and he longs for the entrance of his race into the radiance of the messianic age.

But how can this be? His sense of the divine holiness and the sinfulness of humans prevents any easy solution. The problem of human glorifying is one with the problem of human justification; and the only answer is in the grace of God who in the events of the gospel brings both God's glory and God's justification within reach of human beings. In a number of passages the connection between glory and justification is suggested (cf. Rom. 3:23-24, 5:1-2). Nowhere is the connection more plain than in 2 Corinthians 3, where St. Paul contrasts the two covenants: "For if the ministration of condemnation is in glory, much rather doth the ministration of righteousness exceed in glory" (2 Cor. 3:9). The transitory glory of the old covenant is surpassed by the abiding glory of the new covenant, since the latter is a covenant of righteousness by which justification is made effective.

There is thus in the thought and language of St. Paul a certain fusion between a quasi-physical conception of light and radiance, and a view of the glory as the power and character of God in redemption through Christ. And the former conception seems to be dominated by the latter. Neither aspect of St. Paul's thought can probably be excluded from the pregnant phrase: "the glory of God in the face of Jesus Christ." Here we seem to be at the heart of St. Paul's doctrine. The phrase occurs in a description of the work of the apostles in the preaching of the gospel:

> But even if our gospel is veiled, it is veiled in them that are perishing: in whom the god of this world hath blinded the minds of the unbelieving, that the light of the gospel of the glory of Christ, who is the image of God, should not dawn upon them. For we preach not ourselves, but Christ Jesus as Lord, and ourselves as your servants for Jesus' sake. Seeing it is God that said, Light shall shine out of darkness, who shined in our hearts, to give the light of the knowledge of the glory of God in the face of Jesus Christ. (2 Cor. 4:3-6)

In contrast with the darkened minds of the heathen, whom Satan has blinded, there is the illumination which the gospel brings. The content of the gospel is "the glory of the Messiah"; and because the Messiah is the *eikon,* or perfect representation, of God, "the glory of the Messiah" and "the glory of God" are identical. The illumination brought by the gospel is likened to a new creative act of God. God, who said, "Let there be light" and caused the light first to appear from the primeval darkness, has by a new creation set in the hearts of men and women the illumination brought by the glory of God in the face of Jesus. It is both an external event, as when St. Paul says: "Have I not seen Jesus our Lord?" (1 Cor. 9:1); and an inward act of grace, as when he says: "it pleased God to reveal his Son in me" (Gal. 1:16)....

How great has been the reversal in the attitude of Saul of Tarsus towards Jesus Christ, and how correspondingly great has been the revolution in his doctrine of the divine glory! Here, in the life, death, and resurrection of the Messiah, the hope of the entry of humankind into the radiance of the world-to-come is brought near, and at the Parousia the hope will be more than answered. The anxious piety of the devout Pharisee gives place to a new conviction of the sovereignty and fatherly love of God. Because God is "the God of our Lord Jesus Christ, the Father of glory," St. Paul knows that he lives in a world where the decisive act of salvation has already been wrought, where suffering itself is transfigured, where

> neither death nor life, nor angels, nor principalities, nor things present, nor things to come, nor height, nor depth, nor any other creature shall be able to separate us from the love of God which is in Christ Jesus our Lord. (Rom. 8:38-39)

Even as a prisoner, with the prospect of death before him, he is sure that the sovereign power of God is working out the purpose of his will with the praise of his glory as the goal.

Just because St. Paul was convinced of the revelation of the *kabod* in the Messiah's work of deliverance, he was the more confident in his expectation of the participation of the Christians in the radiance of the "eschatological" glory. The Lord Jesus, risen from the dead, was already in glory (cf. Phil. 3:21), and when he returned in glory his people would enter into the glory themselves (cf. 1 Thess. 2:12; 2 Thess. 2:13-14; Rom. 8:18; Col. 3:4). Such is the hope which St. Paul describes by the word *doxa.* The image is that of the elect dwelling in celestial light. It will be both a glory of Christ which we shall see, and a glory that will enfold us.

The present life of the Christians is therefore lived in reference to the future glory. The thought of the apostles does not begin with the present and pass on to the eschatology as a kind of further stage. It begins with the eschatology, intent upon the coming parousia; and then it perceives that the eschatology is being anticipated in the here and now, and that the glory of the parousia seems to throw its light backwards upon the present life of the church. Paul teaches that there is an anticipated glory wrought in the Christians by the Holy Spirit as an earnest or foretaste of the glory to come.

The classic description of the glorifying of the Christians at the present hour is in 2 Corinthians 3. St. Paul has been contrasting the old covenant and the new: the one is akin to the transitory glory upon the face of Moses, the other is akin to the abiding glory of the gospel. The contrasts made are part and parcel of St. Paul's gospel. If the dispensation of the Law, with the condemnation of sinners as its outcome, was glorious, how much more glorious is the dispensation of the Holy Spirit with, as its outcome, the conferring of righteousness upon humankind.

But St. Paul goes on to make a bolder claim. Here and now Christians can see the glory of God, mirrored in Jesus Christ, and can be transformed into its likeness (cf. 2 Cor. 3:12-18)....

The glorification of Christians is no pious mysticism. It is a matter of conflict and struggle in human flesh and blood. From first to last it is realized by faith; and the receiving of the image of Christ from glory unto glory cannot be separated from the bestowal of the righteousness of God "from faith unto faith" (Rom. 1:17). It includes the imitation of Christ in outward actions (1 Cor. 11:1), and the "formation" of Christ in the inward person (Gal. 4:19). It involves the continual rejection of the standards and values of this present age, in order that the will of God may be discerned (Rom. 12:2). This means a life such as the present age may not deem to be glorious in the least. St. Paul tells us, a little later in 2 Corinthians, what the life in glory meant for the apostles: they were

> pressed on every side, yet not straitened; perplexed, yet not
> unto despair; persecuted, yet not forsaken; smitten down, yet

not destroyed; always bearing about in the body the dying of Jesus that the life also of Jesus may be manifested in our mortal flesh. (2 Cor. 4:8-10)

But amid these conflicts they discovered the true relation between "a light affliction" and "an eternal weight of glory" (2 Cor. 4:18).

The glory is thus hidden from the world and, in a measure, hidden from the Christians who are already beginning to participate in it. But at the parousia it will be unveiled (cf. Col. 3:1-4).

....

The bridge [between the Now and the Eschatology] is wrought by the Holy Spirit whose present activity within the Christians is the earnest of the final glory. The Holy Spirit brings into the present life the powers of the age to come (Heb. 6:4-5). His first fruits are in the Christians, anticipating the final redemption of their body (Rom. 8:23). He is "the Holy Spirit of promise, an earnest of our inheritance" (Eph. 1:13-14). He is the Spirit "in whom ye were sealed unto the day of redemption" (Eph. 4:30). The eschatological context of the doctrine of the Spirit is fundamental: there is no separation between our vocation to the service of God in this world and our salvation unto glory in the age to come, for these are two facets of a single mystery. "The eschatology is active in the present life of the Christians, and the present life of the Christians is governed by the eschatology."[4] To overlook this is to miss the secret of apostolic Christianity.

⤳ 18 ⤳

Glory in St. John

From *The Glory of God and the Transfiguration of Christ*, pp. 57-81.

The Fourth Evangelist records the story of the ministry, passion, and resurrection of Jesus with the conviction that the glory of God was manifested throughout the events. Hidden from those

---

4. Kittel, *Theologishes Wörterbuch*, II, p. 396.

who did not believe, it was apparent to those within the circle of
faith. The Transfiguration is omitted, for the glory belongs not to
any isolated episodes but to the story as a whole....His gospel is
indeed the gospel of the glory.

The prologue leads up to the great affirmation:

> The Word became flesh and dwelt among us, and we beheld his
> glory, glory as of the only begotten from the Father, full of grace
> and truth. (John 1:14)

But this affirmation cannot be understood apart from the opening
verses:

> In the beginning was the Word, and the Word was with God,
> and the Word was God....All things were made by him; and
> without him was not anything made that hath been made. In
> him was life; and the life was the light of men. (1:1-4)

The manifestation of the glory of the Son of God is the climax of
the activity of the Word who was in the beginning with God, created
all that exists, and gave life to the whole creation and light to the
human race. The event cannot be torn from its cosmic context. The
glory which the disciples saw in Galilee, Jerusalem, and Calvary is
the glory of him who created the heavens and the earth and made
himself known in his created works, in providence, in history, and
in the redemption of Israel. All that is learned of the glory of God
from the Pentateuch, psalmists, prophets, wise persons, and rabbis,
and from the light that lighteth every human being, is both fulfilled
and outshone in the glory of the Word-made-flesh....

The Word became flesh. The paradox of the incarnation is set
forth in the contrasted words *logos-sarx*—the abiding Word of God,
perishing human nature. "All flesh is as grass...the grass withereth,
the flower fadeth: but the word of God shall stand for ever." It is
in this paradox that the deepest significance of the glory will be
found to lie. The Word *dwelt* among us. We are reminded both of
the tabernacle in the wilderness and of the prophetic imagery of
Yahveh tabernacling in the midst of his people, and of the *shekinah*
which he causes to dwell among them. The Targum of Isaiah 60:2,
had said: "In thee the *shekinah* of Yahveh shall dwell, and his glory

shall be revealed upon thee." The place of his dwelling is the *flesh* of Jesus....

The Word dwelt among us. Should we translate *en hemin* as "within us"? "Within us" is indeed congruous with the final purpose of the incarnation, for the glory will one day dwell in the disciples. But "among us" must be the meaning here, for the glory of the Word is *seen* by the disciples: it is the object of their gaze, and is not yet within them. The indwelling must await the glorifying of Jesus by the cross, and the mission of the Holy Spirit.

Meanwhile *we beheld his glory.* The author writes as one of the eye-witnesses of the life of Jesus. The glory is *as of an only begotten from the Father* (RSV margin); it is a glory congruous with his Sonship, a glory such as a Father bestows upon an only Son. Neither in history nor in eternity has he a glory that is of himself alone, and in revealing his own glory he reveals the Father's.

The Word-made-flesh is *full of grace and truth.* The Old Testament words that lie behind are "mercy and truth." At Sinai God revealed himself "plenteous in mercy and truth" (Exod. 34:6), and in the psalmist's picture of the divine visitation:

> Surely his salvation is nigh them that fear him;
>> that glory may dwell in our land.
> Mercy and truth are met together;
>> righteousness and peace have kissed each other.
>> (Ps. 85:9-10)

Grace and *truth* summarize the ministry of our Lord as the Fourth Gospel describes it. If grace is apparent in the works whereby life and light are given to those who believe, and truth is apparent in the words whereby Christ makes known what he has heard from the Father, the contrast is not absolute. Grace and truth are present in works and words alike.

To the incarnation both prophecy and law have pointed forward, and by incarnation both are fulfilled. St. John goes on to tell of how both John Baptist the prophet and Moses the giver of the Law yield place to the finality of Christ.

> John beareth witness of him, and crieth, saying, This was he of whom I said, He that cometh after me is become before me; for he was before me. For of his fullness we all received, and grace

for grace. For the law was given by Moses; grace and truth came
by Jesus Christ. No man hath seen God at any time; the only
begotten Son [God only begotten, *RSV margin*], which is in the
bosom of the Father, he hath declared him. (1:15-18)

Here is the answer to the old problem of the vision of God. John
says here that God in himself is invisible, a truth repeated in 5:37,
"ye have neither heard his voice nor seen his form," and again in 1
John 4:12, "no man hath beheld God at any time." But the invisible
God has been declared to humankind by One who is in the bosom
of the Father, God only begotten. And so complete is this revelation
of God that the language of vision becomes in a sense admissible:
even now human beings *can* see God (12:45, 14:9, 15:24). But this
is not the fullest vision. There is a vision yet to come—when the
Son has been glorified with the glory which he had with the Father
before the world began (17:5), and the disciples are led to the
vision of this glory (17:24). The open vision comes only at the
Lord's return, and the last word is said in the First Epistle of St.
John:

> Beloved, now are we children of God, and it is not yet made
> manifest what we shall be. We know that, if he shall be mani-
> fested, we shall be like him; for we shall see him even as he is.
> (1 John 3:2)

The sight of God, wrote Westcott, is the transfiguration of man....
It is in the mutual self-giving of the Father and the Son, expressed in the dependence and submission of the Son throughout
his earthly mission, that the deepest meaning of the glory lies. Jesus
realizes his own glory only as he makes himself as nought in the
quest of the glory of his Father. The contrast is therefore plain
between glory in the pagan sense and glory as Jesus reveals it. Men
and women seek the glory of personal distinction through the
praise and esteem of others: Jesus reveals the glory of self-giving
love which is the glory of the Father and the Son (cf. John 8:54,
5:44, and 7:18). Such is the glory, wherein the Father glorifies the
Son and the Son glorifies the Father, alike in eternity and in history.
Here we touch the heart of the Johannine theology. The glory seen
in the works of Jesus is a glory whose secret the passion ultimately

discloses. It is no accident that the ministry of the signs leads on to the event of the passion:

> When ye have lifted up the Son of Man, then shall ye know that I am he, and that I do nothing of myself, but as the Father taught me, I speak these things. (8:28)

> Therefore doth the Father love me, because I lay down my life, that I may take it again. No one taketh it from me, but I lay it down of myself. I have power to lay it down, and I have power to take it again. This commandment received I from my Father. (10:17-18)....

But with the glory there is the judgment:

> Now is the judgment of the world: now shall the prince of this world be cast out. And I, if I be lifted up from the earth, will draw all men to me. (12:32)

The passion, whose glory is learned only by those who believe, is the judgment upon the world which does not believe. "Lifted up" recalls both the brazen serpent in the wilderness (cf. John 3:14) and the servant of Yahveh who will be lifted up and high exalted (Isa. 52:12). The serpent, hideous to look upon, was the means of healing: the servant with no beauty that human beings should desire him brings deliverance from sin. To the world, judgment; to those who believe, glory: this is the paradox of Calvary.

With the thought of the tragedy of unbelief and the certainty of judgment St. John brings to a close his record of the public teaching of Jesus. Isaiah had foretold the unbelief of the Jews, when he spoke of the blinding of their eyes and the hardening of their hearts at the time when, in his vision in the temple, he saw the glory of Christ. And now among the Jews there are some who believe, even from the Pharisees; but they dare not confess it, for they "loved the glory of men more than the glory of God." Thus has the Incarnate Word divided people, and sifted those who were so bent upon the glory they received one from another that they sought not the glory that comes from the only God (cf. 5:44).

Throughout the narrative [of the passion] John shows that the prayer [of Jesus] is being answered and the Son is being glorified....Calvary is no disaster which needs the resurrection to

reverse it, but a victory so signal that the resurrection follows
quickly to seal it. John thinks of the glorifying of Jesus as completed
on Easter day. The glorifying accomplished, the Spirit can be given
(cf. 7:39). Coming to the apostles on the evening of "that day" Jesus
breathes on them and says: "Receive ye the Holy Ghost." By the
breath of a new creation the church is brought to birth and sent
upon its mission: "as the Father hath sent me, even so send I you."

By the mission of the church the judgment and the glory are
made known to humankind, and the world can take its choice.

∿ **19** ∿

Glory in the Resurrection

From *The Glory of God and the Transfiguration of Christ*, pp. 29-35.

If the greater final significance belongs to those uses of *doxa* in
the New Testament which connect it with the character and
power of God revealed in the gospel, there can be no question of
the greater prominence of those uses which connect it with light
and radiance. In the synoptic gospels, in the Acts of the Apostles,
in St. Paul's epistles, and in the Petrine writings it denotes the
radiant, heavenly state into which our Lord was exalted at the
resurrection and ascension and into which the Christians hope to
enter at his parousia. This eschatological use seems to be the
groundwork of the apostolic doctrine.

In the sayings recorded in the synoptic gospels our Lord uses
the word "glory," apart from a few instances of a "secular" use,
solely in connection with the future. The imagery is akin to that
familiar in the apocalyptic books; but, if in one or two passages
there is a similarity to the language of the Similitudes of Enoch (e.g.
Matt. 25:31), the influence of the description of the Son of Man in
Daniel 7 is more prominent (Mark 8:38, 13:26; Matt. 25:31, 19:28).
The request of the sons of Zebedee contains the word *doxa* in a
similar sense (Mark 10:37). The glory lies in the future, beyond the
passion.

The picture of the Son of Man in glory is no novelty....Scholars are divided as to the primary element in the background to our Lord's use of the title. Yet the *novel* element in our Lord's use of it is unmistakable: "the Son of Man must suffer." It is by a road of suffering that Jesus must enter into the glory which the Father has in store for him as Messiah, King, and Judge. He is *barnasha,* "the Man"—the Man through whose heavenly glory and preceding suffering the kingdom of God comes.

In the latter part of St. Mark's gospel the sayings of Jesus disclose the twofold picture of the Son of Man suffering and the Son of Man in glory. And side by side with this theme there is the challenge to the disciples: if they will suffer, they too will share in the glory.

The eschatological use of the word "glory" is renewed in the teaching of the apostolic church, but meanwhile the event of the resurrection has wrought a decisive change. Jesus has been exalted into the radiant light of heavenly glory; and in the conviction of his Lordship, as risen from the dead and now in heaven, the apostles await with certainty his coming to receive his followers into glory with him.

The glory is frequently linked with the resurrection and the ascension (Acts 3:13, 7:55; Rom. 6:4; 1 Pet. 1:21; 1 Tim. 3:16). The wide diffusion of these passages among the apostolic writings (including one quasi-credal passage) shows how fundamental is the belief that the resurrection was *into glory.* But in these passages the word "glory" has more than one relation to the event. By the power of the Father's glory the resurrection of Christ was wrought (Rom. 6:4). Glory was conferred upon Christ by the Father through the exaltation (Acts 3:13; 1 Pet. 1:21). And into the radiance of the glory Christ was exalted (Acts 7:55; 1 Tim. 3:16). It may be that this last conception owed something to the vision of St. Paul at his conversion, when he "saw on the way a light from heaven, above the brightness of the sun" (Acts 26:13; cf. 9:3, 22:6; 2 Cor. 4:6). The risen Christ is now in "the body of his glory" (Phil. 3:21). But there is no reason to suppose that the apostolic belief in Christ's heavenly glory *originated* from St. Paul's vision, for the conviction that Jesus was now in glory would be an inevitable corollary to the primitive conviction that, raised from death and exalted to heaven, he was "at the right hand of God."

For a while "the heavens must receive him" (cf. Acts 3:21), but at the Parousia the glory which is now hidden will be unveiled, and the faithful will see it and share in it. The Pauline epistles illustrate this hope (Rom. 5:2, 8:18; Col. 3:4). So, with special intensity, does the First Epistle of Peter (1 Pet. 4:13, 5:4). And, if this hope is less prominent in some of the later New Testament writings as a result of a greater emphasis on the presence of Christ, as already realized, it never dies away. Christ's people remain "looking for the blessed hope and appearing of the glory of our great God and Savior Jesus Christ" (Titus 2:13).

Such is the ardent hope of the first Christians. Their imagery is drawn from the Old Testament and the apocalyptic books. It is idle to deny that the conception is quasi-physical. The "inheritance of the saints in light" (Col. 1:12) is a region filled with the glow of a divine radiance. But, as in the Old Testament, the quasi-physical and the ethical are not far apart; and the radiance of heaven is thought of in terms of the ethical contrast between light and darkness, "ye were once darkness, but are now light in the Lord: walk as children of light" (Eph. 5:8). Thus the imagery of glory expresses realities that reach beyond itself. At the center of these realities is Jesus Christ himself; and hence the apostolic writers are concerned not to elaborate their descriptions of the heavenly glory, but to emphasize that Jesus Christ himself is its center. It was *his* resurrection which begat their faith, and it is *his* appearing which awaits them, "on whom, though now ye see him not, yet believing, ye rejoice greatly with joy unspeakable and full of glory" (1 Pet. 1:8).

The glory of the Parousia is, however, anticipated already in the experience of the church. Just as the future does not contain the whole of the truth about the kingdom of God, so the future does not monopolize the whole of the manifestation of the glory. First, there was the growing realization in the apostolic church that the glory, signally linked as it was to the resurrection and the Parousia, was also manifested in the birth, life, ministry, and passion of Jesus. There was also the realization that, though the full and final entry of the Christians into the glory was yet to come, they were already being brought into union with the glory by means of the work of the Holy Spirit. We may quote St. Paul:

We all, with unveiled face reflecting (*RSV margin*, beholding) as a mirror the glory of the Lord, are transformed into the same image from glory to glory, even as from the Lord the Spirit. (2 Cor. 3:18)

And the First Epistle of Peter:

If ye are reproached for the name of Christ, blessed are ye; because the Spirit of glory and the Spirit of God resteth upon you. (1 Pet. 4:14)

Third, there was also the recognition, prominent in the gospel of St. Mark, that during his earthly ministry our Lord had been seen on one occasion by three disciples in that state of light and radiance which would be his in the glory beyond the Passion....St. Mark regards [the Transfiguration] as a disclosure, before the Passion, of the glory which was in store for Christ and for the disciples.

In these ways the notes of anticipation and of realization break into the apostolic expectation of the future glory; and finally the Fourth Evangelist insists that the glory, which the church is destined to behold in open vision, has indeed been already manifested in the historical life of Jesus and perceived by those who believed.

In expressing a future even which has already been in a sense anticipated, *doxa* resembles certain other words familiar in the apostolic writings. The word *Parousia*, which we are wont to connect exclusively with the second coming of Christ, does not exclude the thought of an immediate presence.

Though...the primary reference is eschatological, to a definite coming that had not yet been fully manifested, it is impossible not to notice how appropriate the word was to emphasize the nearness and the certainty of the "coming." So near was it that it was not so much a "coming" as already a "presence" of the Lord with his people, a *permanent* presence moreover, which not even absence from sight for a little while could really interrupt, and which, when fully re-established, would last for ever.[5]

---

5. George Milligan, *St. Paul's Epistle to the Thessalonians*, p. 147.

Similarly those words which speak of the manifestation of Christ
are used both of a future consummation and of the original events
of the gospel....Epiphany, apocalypse, manifestation—the appearing of the divine light, the disclosure of the divine secret, the
coming before human eyes of Christ—these are things which the
Christians await with the conviction that what the future will bring
is but the consummation of a past event and a present possession.
Nor is it otherwise with the glory. As they worship Jesus the Lord
who has been exalted into it, and as they look for the day when it
is made visible, they come to realize that it has been disclosed to
them and is already near to them.

V

JESUS CHRIST

The following selections concerning Jesus Christ are from popular books which Michael Ramsey developed from lectures he gave in various settings. They show him at his best as a theologian who was able to bridge the gap between scripture and the general reader or listener. Holy Scripture, as Ramsey said on other occasions, is difficult for many people because it requires a new way of thinking and believing about oneself and the world. Bishop Ramsey was able to take biblical themes and interpret them for others. He could also transcend some of the controversial areas of biblical scholarship because, while not a participant in the scholarly controversies about Jesus, he was aware of them and could see beyond the controversies to the real subject: the Jesus in whom Christians believe.

What comes through in these selections also is Ramsey's profound belief in the incarnation and its significance for us who do believe. He was always concerned to emphasize the unity of Jesus with us ordinary human beings, while at the same time he could show how the figure of Jesus calls us beyond ourselves into our union with God. Thus, for example, in the selection from *God, Christ, and the World,* which was partly a response to the controversies about the meaning of Jesus and the "death of God" movement, he related the suffering and death of Jesus on the cross to Christian belief about God's glory as God's sharing in our suffering and death. The cross of Jesus, far from announcing God's death, shows God's oneness with us and gives us the hope of glory. This is, for Bishop Ramsey, the ultimate significance of the incarnation.

～ **20** ～

The Claims of Jesus

From *Introducing the Christian Faith*, pp. 37-43.

What do you think about Jesus Christ? *Jesus:* that is a name, like Robert or Richard or Peter. *Christ:* that means the anointed king whom the Jews expected to come and establish the reign of God. The significance of Jesus for the world is bound up with the significance of the Jews for the world. Challenged by them, we have the challenge of him.

God created the human race in his own likeness, in order that it might reflect his own goodness and find free fellowship with him in the recognition of utter dependence upon him. Set in the midst of the world of nature, the human race is designed so as to use and in part to control nature in unselfish fellowship between human beings, and in free and loving obedience to the Creator, "giving glory" to the Creator and coming finally to the vision of him in his perfection for ever. Misusing their freedom, human beings have estranged themselves from the Creator, and entangled themselves in a total dislocation of the right relation between God, humanity, and things. Many signs of the divine image in humanity remain: many gropings after humanity's true destiny are seen. But the human race is impotent to retrieve what has gone wrong, unless God himself acts to set it free.

How does this happen? Jews and Christians believe that it happens by what has been called "the scandal of particularity." The human race has *aggrandized* itself. God, coming to set the race free from pride, *humbles* himself. He humbles himself by a particular action in a particular history, which the books of the Bible describe.

That is where the Bible comes into our theme. Christians say that it contains "the word of God," or "the revelation of God." But consider *how* this is so. Bibles were not rained down in a shower from heaven, some with Apocryphas and some without. No, the books of the Bible were written at many different dates and stages, but within the particular history of a particular people, the Jews, telling of the conviction that in the midst of this history and people God was uniquely making himself known.

In the Bible, the rough and the smooth are inseparable. It is through a human people with its failings and perversities, through a human literature with its partial insights and responses, that we believe the divine word to have been spoken. The deliverance of the Jews from Egypt is believed throughout the story to be a divine act bringing them to freedom and privilege. The law and the covenant given by Moses link together privilege and responsibility. Then comes the series of prophets proclaiming in a crescendo of majestic messages that God is righteous, loving, holy, accessible to the humble soul, the ruler of all history, using Israel as a messenger to make him known to the other nations. Impossible to explain as a psychological rationalization or as a result of intellectual theorizing, the series of prophetic teachings convinces me completely as being inexplicable apart from the prophets' own explanation in the words "thus saith the Lord." True, God has made himself partly known in many religions and cultures: but what is here unique is God showing himself as sovereign Creator who (in the poetic language which alone suffices) humbles himself to lift the simple from the dust. The theme is the sovereignty of God, shown in a particular history, and to be realized in a climax which will affect all history.

Jesus is the climax of *this* story. He is from the Jews. See how important that is for the understanding of him. If anything is historically certain about Jesus, this is: that he identified himself with the revelation of God to the Jews, their Bible was his Bible, their God was his God. But he endorsed this revelation not as complete in itself, but as a first volume in relation to which *he was himself the second volume.*

Study the story of Jesus in the records which we possess: study it with critical conscientiousness, and with appreciation too. I ask you now to notice certain things about him. I draw only upon the earliest records—St. Mark and the portions common to St. Luke and St. Matthew, as I do not want to beg critical questions, or to press evidence unfairly.

Notice first that the theme of the teaching of Jesus is not himself and his own claims. This is striking. His theme is the kingdom, or the reign, of God. God is coming to reign. God's reign is at the door. That is his message. It is a reign to be seen in the works which Jesus does, in the righteousness which Jesus teaches. But Jesus does not preach primarily about himself: he effaces himself in the thought and the service of the reign of God.

It is in the midst of this self-effacement that the claims of Jesus which peep through so unobtrusively are so overwhelming in their impact. He implies that his own place in the reign of God is such that human being's relation to that reign includes their relation to Jesus himself. Here are a few instances. You will find plenty of others: I leave you to do so. Thus: men and women must be ready to lose their lives so as to find them, lose their lives "for my sake." What a claim! Thus again: men and women will one day be judged in a divine judgment, and in that judgment they will face—*Jesus,* and *he* will say to them, "I never knew you, depart from me." What a claim! Thus again: there will be a new covenant, a bond between God and the people, definitive for the reign of God and its coming—and it will be a covenant "in my blood." What a claim! Beneath these claims there lies a secret which peeps out now and then: Jesus is God's Son in a unique way: "No one knoweth the Father save the Son, and he to whom the Son will reveal him." What a claim!

But, above all, there is this. Jesus teaches that all people must repent: they must confess their sins, and pray for God's forgiveness. But in Jesus there is no trace of repentance, no acknowledgment of sin; not for him the prayer, "forgive us our sins." The greatest saints have been most conscious of their sins. Not so Jesus. Without arrogance, without self-consciousness, he is not one to repent, for he is himself the source of divine righteousness, to those who come to him the medium of God's reign. Indeed, where others have died for country, for friends, for causes, for God, Jesus will die in order to lead humanity to be freed from sin and to die to selfishness. What a claim! Consider, consider what claims these are.

Are these claims of Jesus true? If they are not true, then the making of them involves either fraud on his part or a terrible self-deception. Perhaps you are trying the line that you welcome Christ's moral teaching and admire it, but reject his own claims. It seems to me a most unconvincing line. The moral teaching and the claims are woven into one, for both concern the reign of God. I see no escape from the dilemma: either Jesus is fraudulent, or his claim is true. Either we judge him for being terribly amiss, or we let him judge us. That was, in fact, the dilemma that cut through the consciences of his contemporaries.

What was the outcome? There followed the death of Jesus and the resurrection. Just now consider the community of his followers after a few years, and their attitude towards him then. They are towards him, not just as devotees of a leader, or as pupils of a teacher, but as worshipers of one whom they believe to be divine. They pray to Jesus as to God. Remember that these followers are Jewish monotheists, schooled in the belief in one God alone. The idea of worshiping a man is abhorrent to them. Yet such has been the impact of Jesus upon them that they worship him as God. Either they are indulging in monstrous idolatry, or they are right.

So it was that the Christian belief in Christ's divinity began, not as an intellectual theory, but as the impact of experience. To this task Christian minds gave themselves. First, there was the doctrine that God is One in Three. The Christians had already been worshipers of the God of the Old Testament, and had called him Father. Now they believed Jesus to be divine, and in their lives, now lived in the service of him, they felt themselves sustained by a power within them, no less divine, the Holy Spirit whom Jesus had foretold. There was need to think out afresh the meaning of God's unity, and this was now done in terms of the infinite love now known to be God's essence. The early Christians set themselves to this intellectual task: it was their experience which forced them to do so.

Second, there was the doctrine about Jesus himself. Here much imagery was used to convey the belief. Thus, Jesus is the unique Son; Jesus is the divine wisdom; Jesus is the image of the invisible God: "he that hath seen me hath seen the Father." The imagery all strives to express that Jesus is divine as the Father is divine.

But there is one particular image which I ask you to look at closely. It is the image used by St. John which more than any other sums the matter up. St. John writes, "The Word became flesh and dwelt among us, and we beheld his glory." *Word:* it is a biblical term, denoting one who is living, creative, imperishable, divine. *Flesh:* it is a biblical term denoting what is creaturely, frail, mortal, human. Here then is the paradox. The divine Creator has humbled himself to take on himself the entire experience of existence as a human being, in all the conditions of humanity. That is what we call the incarnation. That is the heart of Christian belief.

Is it credible? It is only just credible. It is credible because there already exists the affinity between God and humanity, through men and women being made in God's likeness. This affinity anticipates the closest final fellowship conceivable between God and humanity. Again, it is credible because of the infinity of God's love, with love's power of entering into the experience of another beyond all the analogies of love's power which we know.

So believed, the incarnation is a supernatural event: it is inexplicable in terms of evolution or the hitherto known course of nature. But, though supernatural, it is also rational. It is congruous with the understanding of the world which we have, with reason, been following. We were created in order to give ourselves to God our Creator in obedience, love, worship, total self-donation. We have failed to, and the frustration of our world is the result. God's answer to our need is to give himself utterly to us in the total self-donation of the Word-made-flesh.

That is the meaning of Jesus. We love him as bone of our bone, and flesh of our flesh. We love him because God our Creator is here giving himself to us. In our present relation to Jesus we look up to him as our contemporary Lord; we look back to the act of humility whereby God became man, and humble ourselves before it.

⌁ **21** ⌁

Jesus and You

From *Introducing the Christian Faith*, pp. 45-46.

Is Jesus real to you? There was his historical life which the gospels describe. There is his existence now, risen from the dead. If you want him to be more real to you than you feel just now, you can do far more to let him be so. There is gospel and there is sacrament.

Look at the gospel of St. John. I suggest it because more than any other book it shows together Jesus as he was in history and Jesus in his universal, timeless appeal. Read, say, from chapter 13 onwards, about the last deeds and words of Jesus before his death. Here is a little work for you. It will help Jesus to be real to you.

Jesus still gives himself to us: he so does this that the relation ceases to be external, like the relation of you and someone standing near you: it becomes the relation described in the words: "I am the vine, ye are the branches. Dwell in me, and I in you."

How? First, by the word of Jesus. That means that when you read his teaching, as in the chapters I have suggested, you do not only use your mind, you use imagination, affection, will; you let what you read become meat and drink to you. Second, by the sacrament of Holy Communion. One point about it now. It is *broken* body, blood *poured* or *offered* that we receive as the food of our souls. Broken! Offered! It is the same divine self-giving of which we have been thinking, self-giving right down to death. That is the answer to our pride, and to the world's frustration.

Thus by word and sacrament, Jesus has his impact upon human lives today. It is the impact which St. John describes in the words about which we were thinking: "the Word became flesh, and dwelt among us: and we beheld his glory,...full of grace and truth." *Glory* is one of the great words of Christian vocabulary. It means here the self-giving love seen in Jesus, the very opposite of the human glory of self-esteem or the esteem of other people. *Grace* is the power whereby Jesus makes us different. *Truth* is all that he shows us about God, the world, and ourselves.

～ **22** ～

The Freedom of Jesus

From *Freedom, Faith, and the Future*, pp. 11-14.

Jesus the free man, Jesus the embodiment of freedom: that is one of the ways in which he has caught the reverent attention of many. Recently several writers about Jesus in history have dwelt upon this aspect of him. Taking first as our authority the records in the first three gospels, I ask what aspects of the freedom of Jesus stand out in the story of his life.

Jesus is free from the rule of tradition. He sets its aside, often drastically. You remember the reiterated antithesis in the Sermon on the Mount, "You have heard that it was said by those of old time, but I say unto you...."

Jesus is free from the dominance of conventions. He consorts with those whom respectable society thought it right to shun: prostitutes, profiteers, hated financial agents of an alien empire. He shocked people by this freedom.

Jesus is free from the pressure of life's circumstances. Let me explain. He feels the tragedies of the world around him with intense sensitivity; he shares, he bears the sorrows of his fellows, he is plunged deep into the waters of human calamity. Yet there is in him an inward peace, a serenity, which seems to belong to another world. This is a very significant part of the freedom of Jesus.

Jesus is free from the dominance of the contemporary. He is not one who in rejecting old traditions is ruled by the current enthusiasms of his contemporaries. He is not caught into contemporary movements, the moralism of the Pharisees, or the otherworldliness of the apocalyptists, or the ascetic withdrawal of the Essenes, or the revolutionary aims of the Zealots. Free from his own age, he seems timeless in his appeal and authority.

Beneath these freedoms of Jesus there is an underlying secret. He is free for someone. He is free from self, and free for God.

How does this characteristic appear in the story? It appears in a blending of authority and self-effacement. Jesus wields a tremendous authority, and he speaks and acts in a way which implies tremendous claims. He forgives sins in God's name, he claims to embody the kingdom or reign of God in his own words and actions, he links the reign of God with a personal allegiance to himself, he inaugurates a new divine-human covenant on the basis of his own death, he will be the one in whose presence men and women will one day be judged. These are claims indeed. Yet in the midst of this majestic authority he is effacing himself, he is making himself as nothing; for his center is not in himself; his center is in Another, in the one whom he calls "Father." The self is free from self because it is free *into* another, the Father, God.

How is this apparent? It is seen in the attitude of thankfulness, gratitude, praise, which lifts the self out of the self: the attitude of the worshiper. It is seen in the continual absorption into the Father's purposes and designs: it is meat and drink for Jesus to be making those purposes and designs his own. It is seen in obedience to what Jesus knows to be the Father's commands, right through from the scene in the temple when as a boy Jesus said, "I must be about my Father's business," to the scene in the garden of Gethsemane when Jesus cries in an agony of prayer, "Father, if it be possible let this cup pass from me; nevertheless, not what I will but what thou wilt be done." These are the media of a freedom from self into God.

So far our picture has come from the first three gospels. When we turn to the Fourth Gospel we see the life of Jesus interpreted in a portrait in which one of the key words is glory. Jesus reveals glory. But he does not glorify himself, he looks to the Father's glory, he effaces himself in order to give glory to the Father. He has indeed glory, but no independent glory for himself, because the essence of glory is self-giving love, to live in another and for another.

Such is the freedom of Jesus. Today despite the decline in religion and the widespread rejection of dogmatic Christianity, and despite the dislike of looking back to a past century for guidance, the figure of Jesus goes on haunting the thoughts and consciences of people. The secret is his freedom, but a freedom far different from that which we can easily understand.

It is from the freedom of Jesus as known in history that Christianity draws its doctrine or philosophy of freedom. Christianity affirms that in God alone is perfect freedom, the consistent self-realization of One who is utterly good, righteous, and wise, the "I am that I am." God is free. And God has created the human race in his own likeness with the design that his human creatures, endowed with the rudiments of free will, may through their right use of it come to share in his own freedom in sonship. They will attain this freedom in the knowledge of God, in the doing of his purposes, in self-forgetful love towards one another in mutual service and towards him in contemplation, with him as their center, their goal, and their glory. So it is that the ancient prayer speaks of God as one whom to serve is true freedom, *cui servire regnare;* and the apostle Paul describes the goal of the created universe as the glorious freedom of the children of God.

In Jesus we see not only the free person of all time but the embodiment of divine freedom, for in this life God discloses himself completely and uniquely in time and history. When in his words and actions Jesus "glorifies" the Father and knows that the Father "glorifies" him—not least in the self-effacement of his death—there is revealed the character of eternal deity, love, glory, freedom. In Jesus we see not only what it means for men and women to be free but also what it means for God to be God.

Not surprisingly, Christians see Jesus not only as the image of what freedom is but as the source of freedom to us. This is described in a sentence in the Fourth Gospel: "If you continue in my word, you are truly my disciples, and you will know the truth, and the truth will make you free" (John 8:31-32). It is a relation of close personal allegiance to Jesus, mediated by the reading of the gospels, by prayer, by sacrament, by exposure to the impact of Jesus upon us which is called "grace." Learning from this relationship to Jesus the "truth," about God as our creator and savior and about ourselves as creatures and sinners, we are set in the path which leads to the freedom of mature sonship. The truth shall make us free.

When the apostle Paul speaks of the "glorious freedom of the children of God" he is thinking of the final goal of heaven in which freedom is perfectly realized. In all our thinking and acting about freedom we bear in mind that final reference. The different aspects of freedom which we cherish and realize in this life are fragmentary anticipations of the freedom which is heaven itself. Yet the freedom derived from Jesus begins now. It is here, real, and creative.

⌁ **23** ⌁

Jesus and the Kingdom

From *Canterbury Pilgrim,* pp. 33-38.

Unable as we are to search in the gospels for biography or for diary memoirs, we are nonetheless able by scientific procedure to gain a picture of Jesus in relation to his contemporaries. We ask what are the themes about Jesus which are well attested within a number of strands in the tradition, in sayings, in parables, in episodes. Asking that, we get a picture of Jesus in his various relationships with the scene around him.

Thus, Jesus is one who searches for the outcasts in society and befriends them. Jesus is lonely, cut off from home and family as he pursues his mission. Jesus is vividly conscious of the presence, sovereignty, and graciousness of God in nature and in the lives of human beings. Jesus shows that a new order is here, breaking in, an order which fulfills the scriptures. Jesus predicts judgment upon the Jewish church. Jesus trains disciples to be the nucleus of a new Israel with whom a new covenant is made. Jesus accepts death as his vocation, and he foresees beyond his death a divine victory depicted in a variety of images. By this procedure we gain a picture of Jesus in relation to his contemporaries in Palestine.

Let us look more closely at the central theme, the kingdom of God, and then at the claim of Jesus in relation to it.

Jesus preaches: "The time is fulfilled, the kingdom of God has arrived; repent, and believe the good news" (Mark 1:14). He presents this theme by mighty works and by the teaching of the divine righteousness. That Jesus did perform mighty works is clear not only from episodes describing them but from sayings and controversies about them, including the allegation that he did them by the prince of the devils. But as to Jesus' presentation of the kingdom and its righteousness, we miss its intensity and its originality if we concentrate solely upon passages which describe "the kingdom" as such in parables or otherwise. It is not only that Jesus says this or that about the kingdom; it is that he witnesses with a rare vividness to the nearness and sovereignty of God, in nature and in everyday human situations. God is near, God is here, in sovereignty, in generosity, in piercing challenge. Responding to God's providence people will be trustful and not anxious. Responding to his generosity they will be loving and forgiving to one another. Responding to his sovereignty they will renounce power, importance, claims for themselves. The rich man can no more enter the kingdom of God than a camel can crawl through the tiny eyes of a needle. Why? Because he is too big, he has power, importance in himself and his possessions. Those who approach like children are not too big, the kingdom is for them....

The kingdom is, however, coming not as a general proposition but as a specific event. Sayings and parables show this. Something is happening. Decision is urgent. There can be no dallying. Here is the harvest. Reap it. Here is a precious pearl. Buy it at once. Here is a door. Hurry through it. And all this because "the time" is here, the old order is breaking up, the new order is come. "Blessed are the eyes which see what you see. For, I tell you, many prophets and kings desire to see what you see, and did not see it, and to hear what you hear, and did not hear it" (Luke 10:23-24; cf. Matt. 13:16-17). It is within this vision of fulfillment that the role of Jesus himself is seen.

It is concerning the claims made by Jesus that the contrast is considerable between the outlook of the older scholarship and the outlook common today where form-critical methods are used. It is a frequent contention of contemporary scholars that the titles used in recorded sayings of Jesus—Son, Son of God, Son of Man, Lord—do not belong to primitive tradition but were read into the tradition in the light of post-resurrection Christology....It seems

to me that both for history and for Christology the significant thing
is not a list of the titles Jesus used, or might have used, but the
nature of the authority with which he spoke and the implied claims
about his role in relation to human beings.

The claims are seen in the context of Jesus' own self-effacement.
His message is not about himself. He is absorbed in the sovereignty,
the purpose, and the presence of God. Yet the implied claims recur.
It is Jesus who will accept or reject in the future judgment (Matt.
7:21-22). It is for Jesus that the renunciations of discipleship are
made (Mark 8:35-37). It is Jesus' death that will bring deliverance
(Mark 10:45) and will be the ground of a new covenant (Mark
14:24). His authority was quite unlike that of the rabbis. It was an
authority which caused the crowd to disperse on the day when the
five thousand—perhaps bent upon a messianic rising—were fed,
an authority which cleared the temple at a word, an authority which
led the Roman centurion to see in Jesus a power over events akin
to his own power over his soldiers....

The mission of Jesus both struck at the religious security of
Judaism and avoided involvement in political messianism. It led to
such resentment by both the Pharisees and the party of the high
priests that they plotted to destroy him. Of this there is no historical
doubt. Nor can there reasonably be doubt that Jesus saw his coming
death as lying within the divine purpose, as part of his mission. If
form-criticism warns us against putting weight upon the formal and
systematized predictions of the death and the resurrection, there
remain sayings which show the will of Jesus to accept the death,
his linking of it with a new covenant, and the frustration which he
feels until it happens. "I have a baptism to be baptized with and
how am I constrained until it is accomplished" (Luke 12:50). With
the covenant there is the new *ecclesia*. The disciples were trained
to be its nucleus, and within it the apostles would be rulers. But
their rule would be rooted in a humility like that of Jesus who is
among them as he who serves. When Jesus died, however, they all
were scattered. It seemed the end for Jesus, and the end for the
ecclesia. Then something happened.

Such is the picture of the mission of Jesus which the gospel
traditions provide as credible history. The picture seems to make
sense in relation to its environment, while its originality makes it

hard to think it could be the product of that environment. It seems also that the inevitable reading-in of post-resurrection interpretation does not obliterate the traces of a primitive perspective. Above all, it seems that the traditions, belonging as they do to the church's preaching and teaching, bear the impress not only of a theology but of a person, a person in whom authority and self-effacement were strangely blended. While it seems that the mission of Jesus was a puzzle until the death and the resurrection unfolded its meaning, it is hard to see how the resurrection could of itself have created Christianity without the sowing of seeds in the previous words and actions of Jesus. It was the impressions of the whole, the person, the teaching, the death, the resurrection, which led the apostles to the conclusion that Jesus is no less than Lord, Son of God, the image of invisible deity, the Word who was in the beginning....

How great have been the changes in scientific method and in the modes of theological approach since the day [in October 1923, he says at the beginning of the lecture] when I carried home my copy of [Charles] Gore's *Belief in God* and began a lifetime's study of the historical Jesus and the Christian faith. But after all the changes we still know a good deal about the history of Jesus of Nazareth; and what we know evokes from me, at least, the response: My Lord and my God.

∾ **24** ∾

The Cross

From *God, Christ, and the World*, pp. 41-42.

In the New Testament it is St. Mark who describes the total dereliction and death of Jesus. It was darkness, destruction, and apparent defeat. But St. John shows that because it was self-giving love, it was also glory and victory. The self-giving love of Calvary discloses not the abolition of deity but the essence of deity in its eternity and perfection. God is Christlike, and in him is no un-

Christlikeness at all, and the glory of God in all eternity is that ceaseless self-giving love of which Calvary is the measure. God's impassibility means that God is not thwarted or frustrated or ever to be an object of pity, for when he suffers with his suffering creation it is the suffering of a love which through suffering can conquer and reign. Love and omnipotence are one....

It has been too common for us to talk in a rather facile way about human suffering and the suffering of Christ. We may too easily posit side by side the fact of suffering and the belief in God's ultimate sovereignty. In truth the sovereignty of God is no easy assertion, and the Christian dares to make it only in the light and at the cost of Calvary. Calvary is the key to an omnipotence which works only and always through sacrificial love. It is the Lamb who is on the throne. Divine omnipotence and divine love (in terms of history a suffering love) are of one. And the assertion of this is meaningful when we are ourselves made one with the crucified and in his spirit can say: "All shall be well, and all shall be well, and all manner of thing shall be well."

VI

THE RESURRECTION

Belief in the resurrection of Christ from the dead as the foundation of our hope of resurrection is central to Christian faith. For that reason, perhaps, it is also one of the most controversial of Christian beliefs. It involves questions of history, how we read and understand the Bible, what it is to be a human being, and ultimately what we believe about God. Bishop Ramsey deals with all of those controversial areas in these selections, but he locates them in the context of the wholeness of Christian faith and belief about Jesus, who is the Good News or Gospel of God for us. The resurrection, he says, is the event in which we are shown who God is, and what our response must be, namely, worship.

In these selections also, Bishop Ramsey is concerned to show that our hope for resurrection and eternal life in God is not individualistic in the sense that we can earn or achieve it through our personal piety or good works. The hope of resurrection from the dead is based upon our trust in God's victory. Only in these terms can we hear the significance of the scriptural words "heaven" and "hell": they speak to us of God's final reign over all history.

⌁ **25** ⌁

The Resurrection as Event

From *God, Christ, and the World,* pp. 77-80.

Without the resurrection the Christian movement would have petered out in ignominy and there would have been no Christianity. It is not too much to say that without the resurrection the phenomenon of Christianity in the apostolic age and since is scientifically unaccountable. It is also true to say that without the resurrection Christianity would not be itself, as the distinctiveness of Christianity is not its adherence to a teacher who lived long ago but its belief that "Jesus is Lord" for every generation through the centuries.

The resurrection is something which "happened" a few days after the death of Jesus. The apostles became convinced that Jesus was alive and that God had raised him to life. It is not historically scientific to say only that the apostles came to realize the divine meaning of the crucifixion for them or that the person of Jesus now became contagious to them. Something *happened* so as to vindicate for them the meaning of the cross, and to make the person of Jesus contagious to them. The evidence for a stupendous happening, which the New Testament writers mention, was the survival of the church, the appearances of Jesus in a visible and audible impact on the apostles, and the discovery that the tomb was empty. The several elements in this threefold evidence no doubt had different degrees of evidential weight for different people, and they have such varying degrees still. As to significance, if it were the existential encounter of Jesus which alone mattered, then the empty tomb would have little or no significance. If, however, Jesus has a cosmic meaning with cosmic effects, then the empty tomb has great significance, akin to the significance of the incarnation itself.

Undoubtedly the resurrection faith was in one aspect existential. The belief of the apostles that Jesus had been raised from death

was different from the decision of a jury that an event had happened on the basis of certain evidences. The apostles' belief was
bound up with their response to Christ as living and with his impact
upon them. As St. Paul told the Corinthians, if Christ had not been
raised they were still in their sins, but they had known the resurrection as issuing in their passage from their sins into a new realm
of conduct.

But, *pace* Bultmann, there was another side to the process of
belief. The apostles, for all the existential character of the Easter
faith, were yet at pains to confirm to themselves and to others that
it was a reasonable faith and that there were facts inexplicable apart
from the resurrection. There was not only the challenge of the
existential encounter: there was also the challenge of evidence, the
challenge to explain a number of events and experiences other
than by the resurrection. That was the significance of the *catena*
of evidence cited by St. Paul in 1 Corinthians 15, of the inclusion
of the particular Easter stories with the tradition and of the collec-
tions of stories made by the evangelists. The Emmaus story illustrates the various ingredients in belief in the resurrection. There
was the climax, Jesus known and recognized in the breaking of the
bread and vanishing from their sight: it was the moment of faith
and encounter. But there had been previously the reflection on the
divine purpose in scriptures which the stranger had unfolded to
them on the road. There had been the report that the tomb had
been found empty, and that the discovery had been corroborated
by other observers. There was the corroboration of the two disciples' seeing of Jesus at Emmaus by the news that the apostles in
Jerusalem had also seen him.

I am suggesting not that the Emmaus story tells us exactly how
the Easter faith began, but that it illustrates the apostolic church's
view of the factors in the creation of that faith for the original and
subsequent believers. To value these evidential actors is not, as
Bultmann suggests, to lapse into a worldly-minded historicism, for
the Easter faith, existential as it is, was and is related to evidential
history. Christians believe in the resurrection partly because a
series of facts are unaccountable without it.

Because of the resurrection the church survived so as to hand
down the traditions about Jesus, and in consequence we know not

a little about Jesus and his life and teaching. But that knowledge was conserved because of the significance for humanity which Jesus was believed to possess.

✃   **26**   ∾

The Resurrection and the New Testament

From *The Resurrection of Christ*, pp. 9-10.

The writer of this book remembers receiving something of a shock when it was first his privilege to attend the lectures of the late Sir Edwyn Hoskyns. The lecturer began with the declaration that as our subject was the theology and ethics of the New Testament we must begin with the passages about the resurrection. It seemed to contradict all the obvious preconceptions. Was it not right to trace first the beginnings of the ministry of Jesus, the events of his life, and the words of his teaching? Here, surely, the essence of the gospel might be found, and as a finale the resurrection comes so as to seal and confirm the message. No. The resurrection is a true starting-place for the study of the making and meaning of the New Testament.

We are tempted to believe that, although the resurrection may be the climax of the gospel, there is yet a gospel that stands upon its own feet and may be understood and appreciated before we pass on to the resurrection. The first disciples did not find it so. For them the gospel without the resurrection was not merely a gospel without its final chapter: it was not a gospel at all. Jesus Christ had, it is true, taught and done great things, but he did not allow the disciples to rest in these things. He led them on to paradox, perplexity, and darkness; and there he left them. There too they would have remained, had he not been raised from death. But his resurrection threw its own light backwards upon the death and the ministry that went before; it illuminated the paradoxes and disclosed the unity of his words and deeds. As Scott Holland said: "In the resurrection it was not only the Lord who was raised from the dead. His life on earth rose with him; it was lifted up into its real light."[1]

It is a desperate procedure to try to build a Christian gospel upon the words of Jesus in Galilee apart from the climax of Calvary, Easter, and Pentecost. If we do so, we are professing to know Jesus better than the first disciples knew him; and the Marcan record shows us how complete was their perplexity before the resurrection gave them the key. Every oral tradition about Jesus was handed down, every written record of him was made only by those who already acknowledged him as Lord, risen from the dead.

It is therefore both historically and theologically necessary to "begin with the resurrection." For from it, in direct order of historical fact, there came Christian preaching, Christian worship, Christian belief. Of the preaching much will be said in the pages that follow. As to the worship, the most stupendous change followed the resurrection: Hebrew monotheists, without forsaking their monotheism, worshiped Jesus as Lord. As to the belief, there meets us throughout the apostolic writings a close connection between the resurrection and the Christian belief in God. The God of the Christians is essentially the God who raised Jesus Christ from the dead. In Peter's words they are "believers in God, which raised him from the dead and gave him glory; so that your faith and hope might be in God" (1 Pet. 1:21). Christian theism is resurrection theism. Similarly, Christian ethics are resurrection ethics, defined and made possible by men and women being "raised together with Christ" (Col. 3:1). What is perhaps the earliest known Christian hymn contains the words, "Awake, thou that sleepest, and arise from the dead, and Christ shall shine upon thee" (Eph. 5:14).

The gospel of God appears in Galilee: but in the end it is clear that Calvary and the resurrection are its center. For Jesus Christ came not only to preach a gospel but to *be* a gospel, and he is the gospel of God in all that he did for the deliverance of humankind....

The center of apostolic Christianity is *crucifixion-resurrection;* not crucifixion alone nor resurrection alone, nor even crucifixion as the prelude and resurrection as the finale, but the blending of

---

1. Scott Holland, *On Behalf of Belief,* p. 12.

the two in a way that is as real to the gospel as it is defiant to the world. The theme is implicit in the mission of Jesus as the Servant of the Lord, and it becomes increasingly explicit until John says the final word. To say that this theme is the center of the gospel is not to belittle the life and words of Jesus that precede it nor the work of the Paraclete that followed it. For life-through-death is the principle of Jesus' whole life; it is the inward essence of the life of the Christians; and it is the unveiling of the glory of the eternal God. So utterly new and foreign to the expectations of others was this doctrine, that it seems hard to doubt that only historical events could have created it.

⋰   27   ∿

History and Belief

From *The Resurrection of Christ*, pp. 35-38.

The theology of the apostles sprang not from their own theorizing, but from certain historical events which led them to beliefs far removed from their own preconceived notions. The most significant of the events was the resurrection. What sort of event was this? What in fact happened? What sort of event is postulated by the message which we have seen to pervade the teaching and writing of the apostles?

Clearly the apostles' message rested upon an event of *resurrection* as distinct from an event of *survival*. The distinction is big and important, between a resurrection and the survival of an immortal soul. In the Platonist doctrine of immortality the body dies, but the soul continues its life. Thus, really and essentially, there is no death for that aspect of human beings that is deemed to be of eternal importance; the truth is that "in the sight of the unwise they *seem* to have died." Very different is a belief that the continuing life of the soul by itself is a maimed and incomplete life, that death is real with no semblance attaching to it, that resurrection is the raising from out of death of a life that will be as rich and richer in the unity of soul and body than the life that existed previous to death.

Now the central theme of the apostolic teaching is bound up with the belief not that Jesus spiritually survived, but that Jesus was raised. He truly died. He underwent, so both the gospels and the epistles tell us, the whole fact of death in all its bitterness. His soul was exceedingly sorrowful, even unto death. He tasted of death for sinners, making himself one with them. He took upon himself the reality of death in its connection with sin. The death was real and complete. If it could be said of Jesus that "in the sight of the unwise he seemed to have died" and that his essential and complete life survived from the hour of the crucifixion, then the central theme of the apostolic gospel would be rendered void and false.

Further, it is not only the continuing life of the risen Jesus that matters supremely in New Testament Christianity. For besides the emphasis upon "Jesus Christ the same yesterday, today, and for ever" there is in the apostolic teaching an equal emphasis upon the *act* of God in raising him. It is the *act* that reveals the power of the living God; and the Christian life is lived in relation to this initial *act* no less than in relation to the contemporary presence of Jesus.

Still further, the event upon which the gospel rests is unique, redemptive, creative. It is not that Jesus Christ by surviving death demonstrates that all good people survive it too. The resurrection is far more than an illustration or an example of human immortality. It is a victory uniquely won, and won in order that humankind may be enabled to share in *Christ's* resurrection. It does for us what we cannot do for ourselves.

The gospel therefore postulates as its basis not an illustration of survival but a miracle of resurrection. Its character as a miracle does not depend upon any portentous happenings that may have accompanied it nor upon its being a "bodily," as distinct from a "spiritual," act. The resurrection is a miracle because it is a unique redemptive and creative intervention of God; it interrupts the hitherto normal workings of historical cause and effect and the hitherto normal workings of the order of human sinfulness, and ushers in a new stage in the cosmic process. "It is evident," wrote Westcott, "that if the claim to be a miraculous religion is essentially incredible, apostolic Christianity is simply false."

A miracle may be called an event wrought by God which does not fit into the hitherto observable laws of nature. It resembles in one way the actions of the free wills of men and women which disturb the dispositions of nature; and it resembles in another way the operations of the grace of God in human lives. It is credible to those who, recognizing the potentialities of free will to distort the divine design, do not deny to the living God his own freedom in his work as redeemer. If the resurrection breaks what appears to be law, it does so in order to vindicate another and a higher aspect of law. As a miracle, it is the disclosure of an order of being new, unknown, transcendental. It is, in the literal sense of the word, a "revelation": it unveils a new level of glorified human life.

Yet though it is a miracle in relation to the observable laws of the world that we know, the resurrection is, in relation to the new order that it discloses, natural, inevitable, lawful. It shows us perfect human nature glorified through a perfect response to the Spirit of God. It shows us the goal for which human nature was created, and to which it will be raised when the law of the Spirit of life in Christ Jesus sets human beings free from the law of sin and death (cf. Rom. 8:2). It shows us both the crown of the purpose of God in the scriptures, and the crown of his purpose in the created world, wherein new levels of life succeed to old levels and the series of successions arouses what Butler called "the implicit hope of something further."

The miracle of the resurrection could thus be made known only to those who responded to the new level of spiritual existence which it disclosed. It was not a portent which could be shown to all and sundry to scare them into belief. Westcott's classic words are worth quoting:

> If then the life of the risen Lord had been simply a renovation or a continuance of the former life, subject to the same conditions and necessarily destined to the same inevitable close, then the experience of unbelievers would have been sufficient to test, the witness of unbelievers would have been adequate to establish the reality of the resurrection. But if it was a foreshadowing of new powers of human action, of a new mode of human being, then without a corresponding power of spiritual discernment there could be no testimony to its truth. The world could not

see Christ, and Christ could not—there is a divine impossibility—show himself to the world. To have proved by the incon-
testable evidence that Christ rose again as Lazarus rose again
would have been not to confirm our faith, but to destroy it
irretrievably.[2]

There was in the resurrection a gentleness and a restraint akin to
that which was seen in the ministry and in the passion.

This is not to say that the appeal to historical evidence is
unimportant. On the contrary, the evidence is of great importance.
It may be shown that certain historical facts are unaccountable
apart from the resurrection, and that different lines of historical
testimony so converge as to point to the resurrection with overwhelming probability. But decisive proof can never be provided.
Belief in the resurrection, involving as it does the most strict
historical considerations, involves also belief in Jesus Christ.

The narratives in the gospels suggest that a number of factors
played their part in leading the apostles to their belief. It was not
the news of the empty tomb alone that convinced them: of itself
this news seemed to them to be idle talk. There was need besides
the empty tomb for the appearances of Jesus; and here far more
was involved than proof by means of visible phenomena. There was
the gradual impact of the risen Jesus upon their minds and consciences; and there was the unfolding of the scriptures so that what
they heard and saw became integrated with their faith in God and
his righteous purpose for humankind. The tomb, the appearances,
the converse of Jesus, the scriptures—all these had their place in
leading the apostles through fear to wonder, through wonder to
faith, and through faith to worship. For their belief included not
only a conviction that a certain event had happened, but faith in
the God who wrought it and in the crucified Jesus whom it
vindicated.

---

2. *The Revelation of the Risen Lord,* pp. 11-12.

∿ **28** ∿

Resurrection, Heaven, and Hell

From *Canterbury Essays and Addresses*, pp. 33-40.

M y present task is to consider with you not this intermediate state of grace and patience, pain and joy, but the finalities, heaven and hell. Yet one preliminary theme must prepare our way. It is resurrection. The sequence of the creed reminds us that we should think first about the resurrection of the dead before we think about the life of the world to come. It is upon the resurrection that the Christian hope is based, and resurrection belongs both to our present state as Christians and to the final destiny.

First, then, resurrection is a mighty act of God. Remember that in the New Testament the language used is not of Jesus rising but of Jesus being raised by God. Jesus did not "achieve" resurrection. Rather did he make himself nought, and when all was dark, when human possibilities were exhausted, God raised him by a mighty act of his power. This truth about resurrection colors the whole process of our movements towards our goal, whether in this world or the next. It is not that humanity, even under God's grace, gets gradually better and better and so attains to saintliness here and to heaven thereafter. Rather does the grace of God work surprises, turning defeats into deliverances, "calling things that are nought as though they are," and acting beyond any laws of progress or expectation. We have no rights here, and no rights hereafter. Unprofitable servants at every stage, we know that the Christian life has always the two facets: on the one side there is the God who raises the dead and on the other side there is "faith alone."

Second, the resurrection of Jesus is the prelude to the resurrection of those who believe in him and are united to him by faith and baptism. I need not recall to you the many references to this in the New Testament (cf. Rom. 6:1-11; Col. 3:1-4). Already the Christians united with Christ are raised together with him. Already they are partakers of Christ, possessors of his life-giving Spirit, sharers in eternal life; St. Paul and St. John are at one in affirming this present realization. But there is a "not yet," and a consummation still to come. Though they are already "in Christ" the Christians are still living in this world; they belong to cities, states, and nations. They are involved in suffering, and in sin which contradicts their Christian status. But amid this ambiguous interim they await a future glory. It will be an unveiling in perfection of a union with Christ at present hidden and incomplete. It will be "the coming of Christ," "the resurrection," "the glory." It must be wrong to try to be literalistic about the imagery used to express the inexpressible, for "eye hath not seen, nor ear heard, neither have entered into the heart of man, the things which God hath prepared for them that love him" (1 Cor. 2:9).

Thus through the doctrine of resurrection in the New Testament, with its double strain of something already realized and something "not yet," we approach the doctrine of heaven. Here let the word "glory" guide us in our approach. It is one of the marvelous words of the Bible, for it tells of heaven and the last things and it also tells of human beings and the first things. So it is; God created men and women in his own image in order that they might come to perfect fellowship with their Creator. It is a fellowship of intimacy, love, and knowledge intermingled with awe and dependence as, for all the intimacy, the line between Creator and creature ever remains. It is this blending of intimacy and dread dependence, of human beings reflecting the Creator's character and humbly ascribing all to him, which the Bible describes by the words *glory* and *glorify*. There is the secret of our existence and of our role in the created world, and the clue to our destiny. Heaven is the final consummation of this, for heaven is our finding ourselves in the glory of our Maker.

So we approach the thought of heaven. Let me now quote St. Augustine, in words rooted in the Bible:

We shall rest, and we shall see:
  we shall see, and we shall love;
    we shall love, and we shall praise.
Behold, what shall be in the end, which is no end.[3]

There is "a description of heaven." Let us follow the description through.

"We shall rest." There is in modern religion a strain of discontent with the idea of heaven as rest. Why, we are told, should repose and inactivity be the goal of energetic people? Hence the modern reaction from the phrase "rest in peace" upon tombstones, and the liking for words like "called to higher service." But these modern ideas are not profound, and they belong to a secularized view of religion. How profound in contrast is St. Augustine's word *vacabimus:* we shall have a vacation. We shall cease from our restless busyness, from doing things for the sake of doing them; and, purged of the egotisms of our own activity, we shall for once be passive and in our passivity realize that it is God who works. So in this passivity our eyes will be open, and we shall see.

Videbimus, we shall be freed so as to see God in his perfect beauty, and "blessed are the pure in heart, for they shall see God." It will be a vision glorious and satisfying, the goal for which we were created. And as we see God in his beauty we shall begin to reflect him, for the seeing will be in a purity of love whereby his love becomes our own. This reflection of him will mean that we love, love him and all his creatures.

Amabimus, we shall love our fellows and be serving them selflessly; the second great commandment will be perfectly fulfilled in the realization of the first. Serving our neighbors we shall rejoice in them and with them; and we shall as never before enjoy our fellow creatures. But in the midst of this love, service, enjoyment we shall be aware as never before that God is the giver and God is the goal; and in full circle the heart which has moved from God to creatures will be drawn back to God in praise and wonder.

Laudabimus, we shall praise God, rejoicing to give to him all that is his due. If the Latin verbs in St. Augustine's description have till now served as well as words can serve, here the Latin *laudare* scarcely matches the Greek *doxazein,* the giving glory to God which is the crown of heaven's meaning. Rest, see, love, praise—each leads on to the other, and all interpenetrate *in fine sed non in fine,* in the end which is no end.

---

3. *The City of God,* 22:30.

Such will be a perfection in which the contradictions familiar in our present existence are resolved. At present we oscillate between *possession* and *discovery*. We know at times the happiness of arrival and achievement. But this can soon be dulled, and we set out again to find the happiness of the chase, of search, struggle, and exploration. In heaven, however, the joy of arrival and possession and the joy of exploration are one; for while all is perfect there is within perfection a ceaseless discovery of novelty—it is ever a new song that is sung before the throne. So too we experience here the contrast between *rest* and *action;* rest is enjoyable but it can become boring, and so we plunge into activity, but activity after satisfying us awhile can tire us and make us long for rest. In heaven, rest and action are one; the saints rest from their labors, and their works follow them. Our peace is in the will of God, *semper agens, semper quietus.* So too in our present experience we never escape the antinomy between *worship* and *service.* We speak often of their unity, but we know in practice the tension between them. In heaven worship and service are utterly one. There is "no temple there," for all is worship, and "his servants shall serve him, and they shall see his face." Thus will our familiar contradictions disappear in the glory of God.

As heaven is that glory, there can be no idea of it as a selfish compensation for life's frustrations, or as "pie in the sky when you die." No selfish desires can lead a person towards heaven, as heaven is the very contradiction of selfishness. There is indeed a doctrine of reward in the teaching of Christ. But the good works which win reward are the outcome of God's reign in God-centered lives, and can never be a selfish investment. And the reward to which good works prepare the way cannot be quantitative, as it is the reward of being with God in his presence.

The hope of heaven is one aspect of the Christian hope which the New Testament formulates in more ways than one. Besides the hope of heaven there is the hope of the coming of the reign of God in history. The Christians pray "thy kingdom come on earth as it is in heaven." Since love is one and indivisible there is no separation between the love wherewith we serve humanity in Christ's name and bear witness to his reign on earth, and the love which is eternal life and the anticipation of heaven itself. Thus we cannot pursue the quest of heaven without a concern about God's reign in history, and equally our concept of God's reign in history will be secularized and robbed of depth if we are negligent of the hope of heaven and our present heavenly citizenship.

Just as we cannot conceive the reign of God in history apart from heaven, which is beyond history, so too we are encouraged by scripture and the Christian tradition to think of things terrestrial as not abolished but fulfilled in heaven. This is the significance of the resurrection of the body. It does not necessarily mean the *resurrectio huius carnis* understood by some of the Latin fathers; rather does it mean that there will be in heaven fullness of personal expression, of recognition, and of the characteristics through which people have been known and loved in this present life. *Non eripit mortalia, qui regna dat caelestia.* The doctrine of the *final* resurrection of bodies to complete the beatitude of the saints conveys in symbol the truth that the perfection of the one is inseparable from the perfection of all those who are to be made perfect. The joy of one is incomplete without the joy of all.

Will, however, some be lost? The teaching of Christ in the gospel of St. Matthew ends with a pair of parables of judgment describing the fate of those within and those without the covenant. The first is the parable of the sheep and the goats. It tells of how all the nations, the Gentiles outside the covenant, are gathered at a final assize; and they are judged by their response to the natural law of kindness and charity—a response by which, all unknowing, they have been either ministering to Christ or spurning him. "Inasmuch as ye did it unto these my brethren, ye did it unto me." We learn from this that those who have had no chance of being confronted with the knowledge and truth of Christ are judged in accord with the light which conscience has given them.

But both of these parables of judgment end with a description of loss, the one describing it as "outer darkness" and the other as "the fire of the age to come." Is there a hell? Can human beings, be they believers or be they unbelievers, exclude themselves from heaven?

The credibility of hell rests upon the concept of human freedom. Our freedom is the condition of our human dignity, of our being creatures who are not automata but can will to love or not to love, of our place in a world based upon love and not upon mechanism, of our adherence to an ethical theism. I am free. Rob me of my power to separate myself from the love of God and to shut myself in darkness, and you rob me of the freedom whereby I know myself the child and creature of the Holy Father. This exclusion is hell, the self-exclusion of those who prefer to be isolated in self-love because they want it so to be. Theoretically it is hard to see how the loss can be *eternal*, for, as F. D. Maurice insisted, eternity is the quality of God and of the life shared with him. Theoretically, it could be everlasting. But is it? We have to ask what has been revealed by Christ.

Christ describes the loss and punishment of those excluded from him at the judgment, and the adjective in the gospels is *aionios*, which some would translate "everlasting" and others "of the aeon to come." We are reckoning with imagery, and imagery is poetical. We need not be compelled to take literally the fire and the gnawing worm, nor perhaps the language of duration. We know that there was a tendency in the early church to elaborate the imagery of apocalyptic in the tradition of the word of Jesus, as a comparison of some parallel passages in St. Mark and St. Matthew shows. Yet when full allowance has been made for sayings which are poetic rather than literal and for the possibility of elaborations in the gospel tradition, it is impossible to eliminate sayings of Jesus which give terrible warning as to the possibility of loss and exclusion. Warnings against loss of salvation are there, incisive and inexorable. What the state of loss may be like or how many may be lost, we do not know. It is one of those matters where our Lord seems to give us not definitions, nor answers to our curiosity, but warning and challenge....

Heaven and hell are called the last things. But they are anticipated daily in the here and now. Every act of faith and charity, every movement of heart and mind towards God are anticipations of heaven. The Christian eucharist is a little sharing in heaven's worship, and the Holy Spirit working in us is the first fruits of the heavenly inheritance, the power already of the age to come. So too is hell anticipated whenever people isolate themselves in pride and selfishness and make barriers between one another and their Creator. Our life as Christians is one of conflict and ambiguity; we live under grace and yet sin dies very hard within us. Thus heaven and hell already do battle, and the conflict between them may be raging within our prayers as well as our actions....

Now prayer is characteristic of piety, and it is plain enough that to be pious is not necessarily to be near to heaven. As with works, so with piety. There can be good works done with zeal and energy, and yet there can be in them a self-conscious busyness or a possessiveness and patronage which leaves the doer in the bondage of self and far indeed from heaven. There can be piety which dwells upon our own spiritual state and our self-conscious enjoyment of it, a piety concerned with its own exterior techniques or its own interior feelings, and the devout person can be far indeed from heaven. Philanthropy and piety alike may be nearer to hell than to heaven. But wherever there are works in which God is present through the humility and the charity of the doer heaven is not far off. And wherever there is the prayer of a soul hungry for God and ready amid its own weakness and failure to be filled with God's own charity, the *vacare* being the gate to the *amare*, heaven is very near. So, not only amid the conflicts of the world but within the soul of the Christians as they pray, heaven and hell struggle together like the twins in the womb of Rebekah, and both are near to us at every moment.

VII

THE HOLY SPIRIT

Belief in the Holy Spirit is also, of course, central to Christian belief in God, but the Holy Spirit has always been something of an enigma to us in the western church. We have tended to vacillate between confining the work of the Spirit to the institutional church and believing it to be a wild and unpredictable force. In Bishop Ramsey's time, the work of the Spirit once again became a source of controversy for many Christians because of the emergence of the charismatic movement and a new emphasis on pentecostalism. He responded to the controversies in the way he so often did, by returning to the witness of the Bible.

The selections in this chapter are largely drawn from a small book, *Holy Spirit,* which resulted from lectures he gave in various places. In addition to analyzing the biblical material on the role of the Spirit in the life of the believer, Bishop Ramsey also seeks to show how belief in the Spirit is related to our belief in Christ and how such belief led to the development of the doctrine of the Trinity. In other words, here, as in everything else he wrote, Ramsey relates all things to God: the Spirit in us, the Spirit in the world, and the Spirit in the church are God's work through Jesus Christ. His response, then, to the charismatic movement was the same response that he would give to any other Christian belief: God's work in Christ and the Spirit are one, because both reveal the glory of God the Father.

↙ **29** ∿

The Holy Spirit and Experience

From *Introducing the Christian Faith*, pp. 64-66.

When I spoke at the beginning [of this lecture] about your relation to God, I tried to show that I was not, so to speak, "selling" you something entirely external to you, but describing something already happening *within* your experience. There is the "beyond" and the "within." That is true of all human beings in relation to their Creator. So, too, in the relation of a Christian to Jesus Christ, there is the "beyond" and the "within." In your response to Jesus, your divine Lord, there is the divine within you aiding that response and enabling your fellowship with him. In your attempts at moral obedience, at loyalty, at prayer, at worship, at the duty of thought and inquiry too, there is the divine in you to help your attempts, indeed to initiate them. This divine something within you is the gift of Jesus to you.

Holy Spirit. I have been speaking in these last minutes about the Holy Spirit as we believe ourselves to have experienced him. Here, too, there is a history behind. Soon after Jesus left the visible world at the ascension, there was the coming to his church of the gift he had himself promised and foretold: Holy Spirit. This gift of divine power on the day of Pentecost was accompanied by visible and audible phenomena which assured the apostles by signs and imagery they would understand that the divine power was invading them. It was an intense and catastrophic experience. A rushing wind, tongues of fire: a power beyond human lives invading human lives. In other early instances of the church's experience of the Holy Spirit the emphasis is likewise upon the catastrophic: an invasion of power from beyond.

But even more characteristic are those aspects of the Holy Spirit which suggest that the power from beyond is intimate, personal within the lives of the Christian people. First, we notice that the

Holy Spirit creates fellowship, and is possessed in fellowship. Indeed, the character of Christian fellowship is to be lifted out of self into a common life of sharing in Holy Spirit together. That is what "the fellowship of the Holy Spirit" means.

Next, we notice that the most intimate teaching about the most intimate actions of the Holy Spirit comes in the Gospel of St. John (chapters 14, 15, 16). Jesus is there recorded as speaking of how the Holy Spirit will be at work in his disciples in the days that lie ahead. Notice two aspects of that work. The Holy Spirit will convict, and will comfort.

He convicts. We form ideas and aspirations in our minds. We adopt attitudes. We make moral judgments. These may be correct or incorrect. But, left to ourselves, they will all be inadequate, or prejudiced, or stale, or in need of fresh thinking out or of purging from wrong motives or egotisms. Christians let the Holy Spirit convict them, work within their conscience to enable them to see straight how they stand toward their Creator and their fellows.

He comforts. This sounds nice and cozy, which is what some people suppose our Christian life to be. But there is comfort, and comfort. In the Bayeux tapestry there is a scene in which a column of Norman soldiers is riding, and the Bishop of Bayeux rides behind them prodding the last man with his stout stick, and the caption below is, "Bishop Odo comforts the soldiers." There is indeed comfort, and comfort. It is the *divine* comfort which the Holy Spirit brings, and this means the strength that comes through Christ. Christ's joy. Christ's peace. The joy and the peace of a death to self, the joy and the peace of liberation into the love of God and of others; the joy and the peace which have as their converse the painful defeat of our restless and unhappy pride. That is what we ask for when, as Christians, we invoke the Holy Spirit, the Comforter. It is indeed a deep and heavenly serenity.

Beyond and within—that double aspect belongs to all our relation to God. How could it be otherwise, if God is what he is? The Spirit within enables you to make your response to God, who is both within and beyond. He stirs your conscience to see what your response involves for you in your service of your fellows, whether near or in some far off part of our world with all its suffering. Conviction and comfort—those are the two great gifts of the Holy Spirit to us, and all is summed up comprehensively when Jesus says of the Holy Spirit in the same passage: "He shall glorify me." Not your glory. Christ's glory. More of Christ, less of you. That is the outcome of the resurrection and the Holy Spirit.

⤳   30   ⤳

The Holy Spirit in the Bible

From *Holy Spirit, passim.*

Behind the meaning of the Holy Spirit for Christianity there lie concepts in the Old Testament which form the background for the mission of our Lord and the teaching of the apostles.

"Spirit" in the writings of the Old Testament is not a person or a definable object of substance. It is a mode of describing how the holy God is active in the world which he created, and especially in persons in whom his purpose is fulfilled.

There are two Hebrew words which appear as "spirit" in English versions of the Bible. One of the words is *nephesh*, which means "breath." It is in virtue of having breath within them that human beings are alive, for the breath animates the physical organs. Thus when Elijah prays for the restoration of the dead child of the widow at Zarephath "the child's *nephesh* returned upon his inward parts and he lived" (1 Kings 17:22). By a process of refinement *nephesh* came also to be used of the inner consciousness (Exod. 23:9) or the emotional life (Job 20:3); and in post-exilic times it is no longer specially associated with physical energy, for it now denotes what we might call the "spirit" of a person, in the sense of his or her "character" (Zech. 12:1).

The other word, more significant for theology, is *ruach*, or wind. It is by God's wind that the world and humankind are created and nature is continually sustained. No writing depicts this better than Psalm 104, where all living creatures, including human beings, are described as depending upon God's ceaseless energy:

When thou hidest thy face,
 they are dismayed;
when thou takest away their breath,
 they die and return to their dust.
When thou sendest forth thy Spirit,
 they are created; and thou renewest
  the face of the ground. (Psalm 104:29-30)

There could scarcely be a more vivid account of the dependence of the world upon the constant sustaining action of a Creator who is both beyond the world and deeply active within it.

The Creator's activity in the world extends not only to the continuing existence of his creatures but to their character in relation to God's purpose. Do people sometimes have remarkable powers, gifts, or aptitudes? These are the work of the divine *ruach,* "invading" men and women. To *ruach* are ascribed the physical strength of a Samson (Judges 14:6), the leadership of a Joshua (Num. 27:18), the wisdom of sages (Prov. 1:23), the ecstasy of the sons of the prophets (1 Sam. 10:10). In this way *ruach* is not merely producing a series of outstanding human specimens, but is serving God's righteous purpose for humanity. So, not surprisingly, *ruach* is specially apparent in the inspiration of prophecy. It is by *ruach* that the prophets prophesy, and the implication is that Spirit inspires not only the ecstasy which they sometimes experience but the *message* of which they are conscious and the impulse to deliver it. "As for me," says Micah, "I am filled with power, with the Spirit of the Lord, and with justice and might, to declare to Jacob his transgression and to Israel his sin" (Mic. 3:8). The Lord's servant is described in Second Isaiah as being endowed with *ruach* for his mission to Israel and beyond Israel to the nations (Isa. 42:1).

Not surprisingly, Spirit comes to be used in the prophecies of the future fulfillment of God's purpose. As the words "glory" and "kingdom" tell both of present realities and of a future hope, so too the word "Spirit" comes into the picture of the good things to come. There will be a day of deliverance, and when it arrives Spirit will be manifested in new ways: in a Messiah, in a people, and in the cosmos....

In all these ways we see that Spirit is a part of the Hebrew theology, with the prevailing imagery of wind. Spirit is not a thing-in-itself, or a person-in-himself, or a philosophical entity in itself; it means that God is active in the world. He is a God at once beyond and within, the Creator and Sustainer of creation, manifesting himself in particular events and persons to forward his righteous purpose, and preparing the way for its future climax. Christians believe that this climax is Jesus of Nazareth....

The church exists by the power of the Holy Spirit. Whether as fellowship, or body, or temple, or people of God, it has no existence apart from the impact of the Holy Spirit upon human lives. Inasmuch as the Spirit is derived from Jesus Christ who died and rose again, the church is called to bear continual witness to the history in which the gospel of God is embodied.

The converts were initiated into the church, in any and every place, by the rite of baptism. This rite, administered by the plunging of the candidate into water, involved profession of faith in Jesus as Lord, reception of the Holy Spirit, incorporation into the Body of Christ, and a death to self which was an act of identification with Christ's death, issuing in a new life which was a participation in Christ's risen life. While the rite united the converts with the contemporary Christ through the contemporary Spirit within the contemporary Christian fellowship, it was an act of commitment to the death of Christ once died.

The eucharist was the center of the church's common life. In this rite the Christians shared in the contemporary life of Christ in fellowship with one another. But this life was the life which had once died, the life defined by the broken body and the sacrificial blood. The feeding on the life was possible because in the rite there was the *anamnesis* or recalling of the death. The rite was thus a proclamation of the continuing significance of the saving gospel history.

What is true of baptism and the eucharist is true of the Christian's life in the Spirit. It is a life guided by the Spirit's continuing promptings in contemporary situations, and a life of growth and movement towards future realizations of the Spirit's power. Thus the Spirit leads the Christians towards the full apprehension of that to which they were once for all committed. St. Paul, counting himself not yet to have apprehended, presses on, "that I may know him and the power of his resurrection, and may share his sufferings, becoming like him in his death" (Phil. 3:10). Life in the Spirit is a life of new adventures and discoveries while being a life of continuing witness to the history whereby it has been created.

It is this historical character of Christianity which gives to the church not only the mission of the Spirit but certain media of continuity through which the Spirit acts in the church's common life: these media of continuity include the sacraments, the apostolic ministry, and a tradition of teaching. The church is thus not without visible shape, and this shape is itself a witness to the history of salvation. But while the Spirit uses this shape and the media which constitute it, the Spirit also acts in unpredictable ways, exposing, teaching, illuminating, judging, renewing. The Spirit is still the unpredictable *ruach* of God.

The tension between these two aspects of the Spirit's action has been apparent again and again in the Christian centuries from the apostolic age onwards. There have been times when the Spirit's appeal to tradition has enabled a true answer to be made to tendencies which might tear Christianity from the historic gospel. There have also been times when the appeal to tradition has caused a kind of fossilized traditionalism which, while asserting the creed can fail to witness that Christ is risen; the tensions between what have been called the "horizontal" and the "vertical" aspects of the life of the Spirit have occurred in many forms, sometimes leading to deep cleavage between an "institutional" and a "charismatic" Christianity. What light does our study of the Holy Spirit in the apostolic age throw upon this problem?

It seems that there are three considerations which may be always helpful for our wrestling with this problem. First, the linguistic uses in the Bible are still relevant to our understanding of the ways of the Spirit. We found in our biblical study language about Spirit as an indwelling possession with the imagery of a kind of fluid or substance within people. We found also Spirit as the violent, unpredictable invasion of persons and institutions from without, disturbing, frightening, exalting. Both these uses are relevant for our ecclesiology.

Second, it is a mistake in ecclesiology to dwell exclusively upon one of the images of the church and to press its implications with a rigid kind of logic. Sometimes, in ecumenical circles, this has been done with the imagery of the church as the Body. More edifying is it to ring the changes often between the varieties of ecclesiological imagery—the fellowship, the body, the temple, the people—and to be confined to none. So there can be a more lively understanding of the Spirit and the church.

Third, the study of the New Testament demands that we should always have in mind the eschatological or futuristic aspect of the church. The church is already given, once for all created, nevertheless it does not yet appear what the church shall be. It anticipates in hope the life of the age to come.

We have seen how basic is the eschatological aspect of the Spirit, as the promise and the first-fruits of the coming age. As is the Spirit, so is the church. Its characteristics are once for all given, and it grows in their realization. Ephesians 4 depicts the church as growing to the measure of the stature of the fullness of Christ, and this picture is applicable to each of the "notes" of the church. Possessing unity, the church grows in the working-out of its meaning through many phases of history and cultural contexts, and the story of the church of Corinth is an epitome of the long Christian centuries. Possessing holiness in the call of God and in the Spirit of holiness, the church grows along the way of Christ's holiness. Possessing truth, for Christ himself is the truth, the church will grow in the apprehension of the truth which is Christ. In each of these ways the church's God-given authority is realized in the church's humble recognition of the "not yet." Thus is the church discouraged from making absolute its present apprehension of unity, or truth, or holiness. Yet in each of these spheres the church's ability to learn and to grow is rooted in its continuing witness to Jesus Christ....

[The apostolic age] was an age in which the Christian gospel moved into different cultural settings and found much variety in emphasis and presentation. Amid the diversity of concept and expression the underlying unity of faith is striking. In each of the phases of tradition and in each of the writers we have examined, there is the constant link between the Holy Spirit and the historical events of the mission of Jesus the Christ. There is the constant belief that as Jesus did the work of God in his mission in history, so the Spirit continues the work of Jesus which is also the work of God.

Furthermore, however the *future* role of Christians is formulated, the Spirit is the dominant factor in that role. In the Pauline epistles the Spirit is the first-fruits of the heavenly age. In the Lucan writings the Spirit is the guide and inspirer of the church's continuing life. In St. John the Paraclete mediates the return of Christ to the disciples and brings heavenly comfort in the midst of their tribulation. Those facets seem to be complementary to one another. Whether the Christians look to the past, or to the present, or to a continuing future, or to the end of time, the Spirit brings the power of Christ to them. At every stage in the developing teaching of the church impersonal language about the Spirit appears as a reminder of the background of Hebrew theology, while the emergence of the language of "he" rather than "it"—seen in the Pauline, Lucan, and Petrine, as well as the Johannine, writings—seems a spontaneous realization rather than the pressing of a theory.

This underlying unity suggests caution in the extent to which we speak, as is now fashionable, of the doctrinal "pluralism" of the New Testament. But if we ask the books of the New Testament to furnish a "doctrine of the Spirit," we find that the answer is an incomplete one, for while these books answer many questions they also pose some questions for the church still to answer. Some of the questions came to be answered within the tradition of the church, some of them call for a continuing answer in the church's thought and experience.

ᔌ **31** ᔌ

The Holy Spirit in the Apostolic Church

From *Come Holy Spirit*, pp. 27-34.

Let us look at the broad picture of the church in the apostolic age, and see some glimpses of this new revolutionary doctrine of Holy Spirit and how it is operating.

First, the old impersonal imagery continues: wind, fire, and water. Do not quench the Spirit, says St. Paul. Do not make foolish attempts to put out the fire. The old imagery, physical imagery, is there. Yet the language of personality also appears. The Spirit wills, chooses, forbids, prays, intercedes, grieves. "Grieve not the Spirit," says St. Paul, as well as "quench not the Spirit." The Spirit is personal. And while Spirit in the Christians is the self-effacing go-between, bringing them the consciousness of Jesus as Lord and urging them to say Jesus is Lord, and bringing them the awareness of the Father as they pray, "Abba, Father," he is himself no less personal than the Father and Son are personal. Indeed he is called both the Spirit of God and the Spirit of Jesus.

Is it not here that we see the germ of Trinitarian belief in the church? Trinitarian belief grew not from the speculations of clever people, but from the native soil of Christian experience. We see the beginnings of Christian Trinitarian belief in a phrase like "through [Jesus] we have access in one Spirit to the Father" (Eph. 2:18), or the salutation at the end of 2 Corinthians: "The grace of our Lord Jesus Christ and the love of God and the fellowship of the Holy Spirit be with you." Written into the Christian doctrine both of God and of humankind is what Joseph said to his brethren: "You shall not see my face unless you bring your brother with you." Relationship—human and divine—that is what the doctrine of the Spirit is really about.

The Holy Spirit teaches fellowship: a new note of unity appears in the experience of the first Christians. The note of unity appears in the experience of Pentecost, where the participants are lifted out of themselves into a common ecstasy of praise. It appears also when we read of their being "of one heart and one soul," and in the sharing of their property in common. But the fellowship of the Holy Spirit had a depth of divine-human relationship, a relationship of go-between that we might easily miss in any superficial thought and language....

What is the range of this fellowship? What is its relation to geography and history, to place and time? To know the answer, we have to glance at some of the other characteristic words describing fellowship in relation to the doctrine of the Spirit.

One description is *ecclesia*. The Christians united to Christ by faith and baptism are a spiritual race and nation, the new Israel whose unity is basically that of the fellowship of spiritual race—in Peter's words, an elect race, a holy nation, a priesthood for God's own possession. So that the *ecclesia* in any place—the *ecclesia* in Corinth, the *ecclesia* in Philippi, the *ecclesia* in New York—means the one Christian people as manifested in Corinth, Philippi, or New York, the members of the race who happen to be living there.

Another word is *soma*, body, and this word speaks more intimately of the union of Christians with Christ and with one another. As the Body of Christ, the Christians are the organ of Christ in the world. In one Spirit we were all baptized into one body, and all made to drink of one Spirit. And as participation in the Holy Spirit involves participation in and with one's fellow Christians in union with Christ, so the growing together and growing up of the members of the body means their growing into the fullness of Christ's own life, growing into Christlikeness so that Christ will one day be totally manifested in those who are his members....

There is a contrast between the liveliness of the apostolic age, when it was exciting to be a Christian, with the miraculous gifts that were a part of that liveliness, not least the gifts of healing, and the sometimes dull, static character of contemporary church life. But just because the Spirit is the Spirit of Jesus, every gift that belongs to the life of Jesus himself is a mighty gift of the Holy Spirit—love, patience, wisdom, courage, self-sacrifice. And when we hear the words, "Ye shall do greater things than these," the greater works that the apostles and their successors are going to do in Christ's name, we remember not only how Christ healed the sick, but also how, in patience and love, he could use suffering and let suffering be transfigured. Let that gift not be forgotten—that when suffering overwhelms a Christian he or she can, in the power of Christ crucified, use it to be, in a creative way, what reflects Christ's glory.

> For you have not received the spirit of slavery to fall back again into fear, but you have received the spirit of sonship whereby we cry, "Abba, Father." It is the Spirit himself bearing witness with our spirit that we are children of God. And if children, then heirs of God and joint heirs with Christ, provided that if we

suffer with him we shall also be glorified with him. (Rom. 8:15-17)

Glorified with him. This last phrase reminds us of an aspect of the Holy Spirit so fundamental that perhaps I ought to have mentioned it first of all, but let me close with it. Call it, if you will, the eschatological aspect of the Spirit. The Spirit is the first install-ment within our present life of heaven which awaits us. The Holy Spirit is, in St. Paul's phrase, the *arrabon*. In another phrase of St. Peter, he is "the Spirit of the glory." In the striking language of the Epistle to the Hebrews, the Christians are those who have "tasted the heavenly gift, become partakers of the Holy Spirit, tasted the goodness of the word of God and the powers of the age to come." In a word, the Spirit enables Christians to live already in the perspective of heaven.

The Spirit keeps this perspective of heaven alive in us as, day by day, he inspires us in the practical service of humanity. We do not indeed forget the relation of the Holy Spirit to suffering humanity, for we think of how the Messiah, at the opening of his ministry at the synagogue at Nazareth, said, "The Spirit of the Lord is upon me, because he has anointed me to preach good news to the poor, to proclaim release to the captives, recovering of sight to the blind, and to set at liberty the oppressed, and to proclaim the acceptable year of the Lord." But every act of love that the Spirit inspires and every prayer to the Father which the Spirit prompts are an antici-pation already of heaven, where every act will be love and every word will be adoration. Faintly, unknowingly, the old writer of Ecclesiastes foreshadowed the apostolic doctrine of the Holy Spirit when he wrote the mysterious sentence: "He hath set eternity in their heart."

॰: **32** ॰

The Holy Spirit in St. John

From *Holy Spirit*, pp. 89-99.

The teaching of the Fourth Gospel concerning the Holy Spirit has behind it not only the theological insight of its author and the traditions on which he draws, but also the church's continuous experience of the Holy Spirit in the apostolic age. Without the experience it is doubtful whether such a book could ever have been written, as it presupposes a Christianity which is lively, creative, and able to move fearlessly into new cultural environments. The conflict between the church and the world had been happening wherever the gospel had spread; and, though the word "Paraclete" may never have been used in earlier Christian writings, the tasks assigned to the Paraclete of witnessing to Christ, convicting the world, comforting the disciples, glorifying Christ, were part of the history of the apostolic age. The Fourth Evangelist is not only expounding a particular theology for the needs of a particular situation; he is witnessing to experience and to ideas already apparent in the church.

Nonetheless, the Fourth Gospel has its own context, purpose, and standpoint, for it was written to meet the needs of a specific Christian community. While there have always been those who have argued for the Jewish associations of this gospel, the main trend of scholarship has been towards an emphasis upon its Greek environment. That environment was at least in part a gnostic kind of religion. Thus there is the contrast between the realm of spirit and the realm of flesh, the realm of light and the realm of darkness. There is the quest for knowledge. There is the "myth" of the savior who descends from the realm of spirit into the world and, after conquering the evil one, returns whence he came. But, as with St. Paul, so with the Fourth Evangelist, the differences from gnosticism are profound....

To come to God, to know the truth, to receive the Spirit, to pass from darkness to light, depends not upon deliverance from the flesh into a spirit realm, but upon the historical mission of Jesus the Messiah who lived and died in the flesh. True, it is fatal to trust in the flesh, or to regard the flesh as sufficient, for "nature" cannot redeem itself, and it is by the power of the Spirit that deliverance comes. The Spirit alone gives life. But the action of the Spirit is derived from the mission of Jesus in history; and history matters supremely to the Fourth Evangelist, ready as he is to interpret its meaning rather than to narrate it as a chronicler.

The theme of the Holy Spirit in the Fourth Gospel is drawn out in three phases. First, there is the Holy Spirit in the mission and teaching of Jesus in Galilee and Judea. Second, there is the teaching in the last discourse at the supper. Third, there are the references to the gift of the Holy Spirit in the narratives of the passion and the resurrection.

St. John (as we will call the author without prejudging his identity) does not describe the baptism of Jesus. But he tells how the Baptist testifies that Jesus is the one upon whom the Spirit descends and the one who will in turn bestow the Spirit (John 1:32-34). So endowed with the Holy Spirit, Jesus pursues his mission; and whereas in the synoptics his theme is the kingdom of God, his theme in John is life, light, glory. Meanwhile there is in John, as in the synoptics, reticence about the Spirit in the teaching of Jesus. Indeed there are only three significant occasions of teaching before we come in chapter 7 to the episode which can be called the "crunch." These episodes are:

1. The private dialogue with Nicodemus that is found in chapter 3;

2. The private dialogue with the woman of Samaria that is found in chapter 4; and

3. The reference to the Spirit at the end of the teaching on the Bread of Life that is found in chapter 6.

1. Nicodemus

Nicodemus, a Pharisee, comes to Jesus by night. Perhaps he is attracted by what he knows of Jesus and wants to express appreciation and the desire to know more, and to combine new knowledge with what he knows already. But the reply of Jesus cuts right across Nicodemus's approach. A new order is here, calling for rebirth, and without rebirth a person cannot enter the kingdom of God. Nicodemus is smitten with incredulity, and Jesus continues the theme; without rebirth by "water and spirit" a person cannot even *see* the kingdom of God. The mention of water no doubt relates the teaching to the sacrament of baptism; but the emphasis is upon the character of the rebirth by the power of the Spirit, as mighty and mysterious as a gale of wind (3:5-8).

Still incredulous, Nicodemus is told that, wonderful though these things are, they are "earthly"; they belong to the rudiments, in contrast with the "heavenly things" which will follow. To these Nicodemus is finally directed—and what are they?

> And as Moses lifted up the serpent in the wilderness, so must the Son of man be lifted up, that whoever believes in him may have eternal life. (3:14-15)

The gift to the believer of eternal life, which is no doubt equivalent to entrance into the kingdom of God, will turn upon the crucifixion of Jesus. Nicodemus came to witness this. Few things are more moving in the narrative of this gospel than the reappearance of Nicodemus to assist in the burial of Jesus:

> Nicodemus also, who had at first come to him by night, came bringing a mixture of myrrh and aloes, about a hundred pounds' weight. (19:39)

So he begins to see the kingdom of God!

2. The Woman of Samaria

The second episode concerning the Spirit is also in private. Jesus is in Samaria, by Jacob's well at Sychar, and being thirsty he asks a strange, local woman to give him a drink. She is astonished at being spoken to in this way by a Jew, for Jews and Samaritans are deeply estranged. But Jesus moves into another plane and says:

> If you knew the gift of God, and who it is that is saying to you, "Give me a drink," you would have asked him, and he would have given you living water. (4:10)

Bewildered, the woman continues the talk on the original plane; but Jesus continues (4:13-14). The woman longs for this water; but her thoughts are still on the natural plane. But Jesus was speaking to her about the Spirit, and the Spirit is the *arrabon* of eternal life.

As with St. Paul and the earlier traditions, here too the eschatological note sounds throughout the doctrine of Spirit. But whereas in the earlier traditions Spirit is the foretaste of the future glory when the Lord returns, in John the Spirit is the pointer to the eternal life available when once the Son of Man has been glorified.

The conversation continues....Jesus speaks of the new order (4:21-24). As not seldom in the gospel tradition the new order is both here and to come; the double stance, however, finds special vividness in the phrase which recurs in this gospel: "The hour is coming, and now is" (cf. 4:23, 5:25, 16:32). And the hour brings a worship in which neither Zion nor Gerizim will have a special place, because it will be worship "in spirit and truth." And this, because God is Spirit.

That God is Spirit is a notion which is found both in the Old Testament and in Hellenistic religion. He is immaterial, in contrast with all visible objects; but in the Old Testament there is the further thought of his power as creator and ruler of the world. Truth is also a Hellenistic concept, but no less a biblical one, for Yahweh is the God of truth. More important, however, than both the Greek and the biblical background is the Johannine teaching that Jesus is himself the truth as well as the way and the life; and the Paraclete whom he sends is named the Spirit of Truth (14:6, 15:26). Worship in the new order brought by the Messiah will be worship freed from the domination of particular sites and buildings, not because of an anti-material "inwardness" but because the new order belongs to God who is Spirit and to Jesus who is truth.

3. The Bread of Life

The third dialogue about Spirit comes at the end of the discourse on the Bread of Life. Here Jesus is in dialogue not with an individual person, but with a number of hearers, first bewildered Jews and then no less bewildered disciples.

The exposition of the Bread of Life has tried the hearers of Jesus very highly. First, he speaks of the true Bread, then he identifies himself with this Bread, and finally he defines the Bread as his flesh, to be given "for the life of the world." The Jews react with horror, and ask, "How can this man give us his flesh to eat?" And Jesus goes further and says that the person who would receive eternal life must eat his flesh and drink his blood. Many of the disciples murmur and in answer to their murmuring Jesus says:

> Do you take offense at this? Then what if you were to see the Son of man ascending where he was before? It is the spirit that gives life, the flesh is of no avail; the words that I have spoken to you are spirit and life. (6:61-63)

These words disclose the heart of Johannine doctrine. Is the eating of the flesh of the Son of Man an incredible idea? Something as startling is to happen—the ascension of the Son of Man to heaven where he was before. But these happenings, both the feeding upon Christ and the ascension of Christ to heaven, belong to the life-giving Spirit and without the Spirit they are nothing. The words of Jesus are Spirit and life; they are filled with the power of the Spirit and they are life-giving in effect.

What is here said seems to apply both to the mission of the Christ and to the eucharistic gift. Both involve flesh, the flesh of history and the flesh of material food. Both are nothing without the Spirit's power.

In each of the three dialogues about the Spirit there has been a looking forward, an eschatological note; now we pass on to the episode where the clue is found.

Jesus is in Jerusalem at the time of the Feast of Tabernacles, the feast which included the pouring of water on the temple steps while the words were recited: "With joy you will draw water from the wells of salvation" (Isa. 12:3). Jesus uses the occasion for some prophetic words:

> On the last day of the feast, the great day, Jesus stood up and proclaimed, "If any one thirst, let him come to me and let him who believes in me drink. As the scripture has said, 'Out of his heart shall flow rivers of living water.'" Now this he said about the Spirit, which those who believed in him were to receive; for as yet the Spirit had not yet been given, because Jesus was not yet glorified. (7:37-39)

The word "given" has no equivalent in the Greek text, which is *pneuma,* "spirit not yet." But "given" is obviously to be understood. In this one sentence we have the key to the Johannine doctrine. Jesus is predicting the gift of the Spirit to the believer, but first he must be glorified by his death on the cross. Death, glory, Spirit: that is the sequence.

That the Spirit is primarily the gift of Jesus crucified and risen has been familiar in the earlier traditions. It is this theme which the Fourth Gospel draws out in the concept of glory.

Glory is a keynote of the Fourth Gospel. God's glory is his splendor, majesty, character, power. "The word became flesh and dwelt among us...we have beheld his glory" (1:14). The divine glory is shown forth in the birth and mission of Jesus, and the narrative of the gospel traces its manifestation in the signs which he performs and the teaching which he gives. But as the story proceeds, a strange elusiveness about the glory appears. Jesus does not glorify himself, he does not have a glory of his own, he glorifies the Father, and in turn the Father glorifies him:

> If I glorify myself, my glory is nothing; it is my Father who glorifies me. (8:54)

> He who speaks on his own authority seeks his own glory; but he who seeks the glory of him who sent him is true, and in him there is no falsehood. (7:18)

For the glory which Jesus reveals is the eternal glory of self-giving love wherein the Father glorifies the Son and the Son glorifies the Father: it is this glory which is being disclosed in the mission of Jesus in history.

There is thus a sharp contrast and conflict between divine glory as Jesus discloses it, and human glory as we understand it. Indeed the contrast is a linguistic one, for in ancient secular Greek the word *doxa* meant a man's personal distinction or status, or the honor which others give to him; whereas in biblical Greek it meant the divine power and splendor—now identified in the Fourth Gospel with divine self-giving love. In a single poignant sentence Jesus is recorded as diagnosing the conflict:

How can you believe, who receive glory from one another and
do not seek the glory that comes from the only God? (5:44)

These are piercing words. The people did not believe, for they were
so preoccupied with the false glory of status and the dignity which
human beings seek for themselves and ascribe to one another that
they did not recognize or desire the true glory which Jesus was
bringing to them. The irreconcilable conflict is exposed.

The conflict between divine glory in Jesus and false glory in
human beings leads on to the passion. In their concern to preserve
national and ecclesiastical status undisturbed, the chief priests plot
the destruction of Jesus. But in the events which culminate in the
crucifixion the divine glory shines. The hour comes when the Son
of Man is glorified.

So the bestowal of the Spirit upon the believers is now possible.
If the manifestation of divine glory in Jesus is the first chapter, the
second chapter is the giving of the glory to the disciples (cf. 17:22).
This is the work of the Holy Spirit: a work whose many aspects are
drawn out in the discourse at the supper and whose deepest
meaning is seen in the sentence, "He shall glorify me" (16:14).

As Jesus glorified the Father in his mission on earth, so the Spirit
will glorify Jesus in the lives of those who believe.

∿ 33 ∿

The Spirit and the Triune God

From *Holy Spirit*, pp. 118-120.

It was once fashionable to derive the doctrine of the triune God
from proof texts like the trinitarian blessing in 2 Corinthians
13:14, or the command to the disciples in Matthew 28:19 to baptize
in the threefold name. Few theologians today would follow that
procedure. One reason is that critical opinion, even of a very
moderate kind, would question the authenticity of the saying in
Matthew 28:19 in its present form. But a deeper reason is that
theologians have come to think of revelation not as the utterance

of propositions about God but as God's self-disclosure through events, the impact of the events upon those who experience them, and the interpretation of those events in the Christian community. Thus it is held that the first Christians began with the monotheism of Israel and, without abandoning that monotheism, were led by the impact of Jesus upon them to worship Jesus as divine, and were aware that divine Spirit within them enabled both their access to God as Father and their response to Jesus as Lord....

Often we have noticed that the Holy Spirit is described as the Spirit of God and the Spirit of Jesus. Yet to say only that the Spirit is the impact of God or the impact of Jesus is to do less than justice to the Christian experience, for the Holy Spirit was felt to be one who from within the Christians' own lives makes response to Jesus and to the Father. "Deep answers unto deep. The deep of God above us and around us is inaudible save as it is answered by the deep of God within us."[1] It is here that the doctrine of the triune God begins to emerge, not only as a mode of the divine activity but as a relationship within the life of deity.

In knowing "the grace of the Lord Jesus Christ and the love of God and the fellowship of the Holy Spirit" (2 Cor. 13:14), and in having access through Jesus "in one spirit to the Father" (Eph. 2:18), the Christians were encountering not only their own relation to God but the relation of God to God. When the Spirit cries in us, "Abba, Father" and prompts us to say, "Jesus is Lord," there is God within responding to God beyond. The Fourth Gospel takes the further step of suggesting that the divine relationship known in the historic mission of Jesus and its sequel reflects the being of God in eternity. Here the key is found in John's concept of the glory. The glory of self-giving love in the passion and the mission of the Paraclete is one with the glory of God before the world began.

---

1. A quotation from W. P. duBose, *The Gospel in the Gospels*, pp. 224-226. Ramsey comments here, "I am glad to recall gratefully this creative theological thinker and teacher in the American Episcopal Church."

~: 34 ~

The Spirit and the World

From *Holy Spirit*, pp. 121-131.

Throughout our study it has been apparent that, in the apostolic age, the language about the Holy Spirit was concentrated within the orbit of the mission of Jesus and the community of believers who were themselves the beginning of the new creation and the heirs of the world to come. The term "Holy Spirit" is never used of the activity of God in the wider sphere of the created world, so intense is the concentration upon the new order which the gospel has inaugurated. It is the eschatological note which predominates: Holy Spirit is the power of the age to come, breaking into the last phase of human history.

The first Christians, however, for all the intensity of their experience of the Holy Spirit in the *ecclesia*, had not abandoned the belief that God was the world's creator, active within it, and making himself known to the minds and consciences of men and women. They would not repudiate the Old Testament teaching about the divine *ruach*, nor the teaching of the Wisdom writers about the operations of the divine wisdom such as the book of Proverbs or the Book of Wisdom describes....

In the church of the early centuries it was the tendency to continue the terminology found in the New Testament writings. The Greek and Latin fathers, when they wrote of the activity of God in nature or in pagan philosophy, would use the term *Logos* rather than Spirit. Such was the concentration of the church upon the sphere of redemption and often upon hostility to the world, that a Christian concern about the presence of God in nature was often far to seek. Where a Christian joy in nature found expression, as in Clement and Origen in Alexandria and Basil and Gregory of Nyssa in Cappadocia, the word "Spirit" was not the word they used. St. Basil could write, "I want creation to thrill you with such wonder that everywhere every tiny plant may remind you of its neighbor" (*Discourse* 9:1); and modern theologians have been surprised that the word Spirit does not occur.

If, superficially, it seems that both the New Testament and the early church encourage a dichotomy of terms, "Spirit" for God's action in the *ecclesia* and "the Word" for God's action in the world, it would be a serious mistake to leave the question there. Neither scripture nor the early church encourages a departmentalizing of the activity of Father, Son, and Spirit; both emphasize strongly the unity of God. God, Father and Son and Spirit, is at work as creator; God, Father and Son and Spirit, is at work as redeemer. The Old Testament language about the action of *ruach* in the world is not abrogated, nor is the identification of Spirit and Wisdom. As the action of Christ in the church includes the Spirit's kindling of the believers' responses, so the action of the Word in the world will include the Spirit's kindling of human responses.

The issue therefore is not one of terminology, or of persons of the triune God. It is the issue of the relation between the action of God in the *ecclesia* as the eschatological community upon which the New Testament doctrine of the Spirit is concentrated, and the action of God in the created world near and far. It is the continuing task of theology to think out as far as possible the relation between these two spheres, and the task is made both more feasible and more necessary by the enhanced knowledge of nature in the modern world.

It is here possible to do no more than to indicate some of the problems, and to ask what light is cast upon them by our study of the Holy Spirit. There is the question of the sciences, the question of the world religions, and the question of diffused goodness in the human race.

As God is the author of all truth and the source of every quest for truth in the human race, the sciences are disclosures of his truth. So truth disclosed in certain of the sciences can illuminate the Christians' understanding of God's revelation of himself in Holy Scripture. Thus the advance of evolutionary biology has enabled a new understanding of the wonder of divine creation as a process through many stages of nature, with humanity as the climax. So too the advance of historical science and literary criticism has enabled

Christians to perceive God's self-revelation in the Bible not only through literalistic statements but through a variety of literary media: drama, poetry, myth, symbol, as well as history. But while the sciences serve God's truth, there can be "mythologies" in connection with them which disturb truth, such as myths of "inevitable progress" or "the scientific mind." If the sciences illustrate the Johannine concept of the light that lightens every human being, they do not reveal or discover what is revealed when the Word became flesh and dwelt among us, nor do they supersede what St. Paul called the wisdom of the cross.

The greater involvement of the adherents of the world's religions with one another is bringing to an end the isolationism which used to prevail. The Christians find themselves approaching other religions with reverence and humility. Taught by the Johannine prologue they will know that in the other religions there is truth and goodness derived from the light that lightens every person. At the same time the Christians believe that Jesus is the perfect revelation of God, the fulfillment of all that is true, the final Word. Christians are likely to witness to this if their concern is less to promote Christianity as a system than to show Christ and to find Christ. The missionary brings Christ to those of other faiths while he or she is awake to finding Christ there. It is thus that they may help people to acknowledge as Lord and Savior the Christ who has been among them.

The diffused goodness seen in the human race is often a challenge to the exclusiveness of Christian language about the Holy Spirit. It is asked whether or how the goodness of those who conscientiously respond to the best that they know differs from the goodness of those who respond in faith to Jesus Christ and invoke the Holy Spirit. Here I mention only one consideration which our study of the Holy Spirit will have suggested. Goodness has God as its author and to belittle any goodness may be to blaspheme the divine Word who is its author. Yet, for the world's salvation, it is the work of the Holy Spirit not only to produce goodness in human lives but to lead human lives to acknowledge God as the author of goodness and to glorify Christ. The life of salvation is the life whose goodness is humbled in the presence of him who is its author and its goal.

So these three issues are raised by the relation of the Spirit in the *ecclesia* and the Spirit in the world....Each of these issues calls for the uninhibited recognition of the divine Word, and therefore Spirit, in the world, and also for the acknowledgment of a divine Savior without whom neither science, nor religion, nor goodness, can climb to heaven—for heaven is the perfect sharing in the glory of God through the Spirit. The pattern of our answer will still be the pattern of the prologue: that the world was created through the Word, that in him was life and the life was the light of men and women, and that the Word was made flesh and they saw his glory. But this answer is credible only when it is reflected in the humility, the penitence, the compassion, the integrity of those who belong to Christ. It is thus, and only thus, that the Paraclete takes "what is mine" and declares it to the disciples....

The Spirit's renewal of the church is linked with the Spirit's witness to the life, death, and resurrection of Jesus. The way of truth along which the Paraclete leads is always the way that is Christ himself, as he takes the things of Christ and declares them to the disciples.

At the present time there are attempts to understand Christian spirituality as an experience somewhat apart from the historical events of the gospel. Our study has shown how in the apostolic age the events and the experience are interwoven. No account of the experience is more vivid than that which St. Paul gives in the opening section of Romans 5. The Christians are justified by faith, they have peace with God, they rejoice in hope, and they rejoice even in suffering, because the love of God was poured into their hearts by the Spirit. But what is this love of God? It is the love made known in the death of Christ for the sake of the ungodly, and in that death the love of God himself was commended to all. The event of the death of Christ not only enables the Christian life, it provides its continuing motive and interpretation. "It is folly," wrote Baron von Hügel, "to attempt the finding of a shorter way to God than that of the closest contact with his own condescension."

But it is a costly thing to invoke the Spirit, for the glory of Calvary was the cost of the Spirit's mission and is the cost of the Spirit's renewal. It is in the shadow of the cross that in any age of history Christians pray: Come, thou holy Paraclete.

VIII

SUFFERING AND
TRANSFIGURATION

S uffering is certainly one of the great mysteries of human life.
"Why does God allow suffering?" is one of the questions most
frequently asked by Christians and non-believers. In these selections Bishop Ramsey approaches this question from several direc-
tions. First, he relates the sufferings of human beings to the mystery
of Christ's own suffering, in which we are shown that the suffering
of Christ on the cross is the sign of God's love for us. God is not
an aloof monarch in the heavens. God enters into the suffering of
humanity; God is revealed as God in the event of the cross.

Second, he raises the theological question of suffering in God
as it was dealt with by his theological mentor, William Temple. He
finds in Temple a movement toward accepting the reality of suffering in God because of what is shown to us of God in the suffering
of Christ. The Christ who suffers is the Incarnate One who allows
us to believe that God suffers with us.

And finally, he writes of the transformation of human suffering.
In his last book, *Be Still and Know*, Bishop Ramsey returns once
again to Karl Barth, who wrote that in Christ our suffering is no
longer a "passive perplexity," but is transformed into that which is
creative and full of promise. Also, Bishop Ramsey returns to the
theme which so often dominated his thinking and his praying:
transfiguration into glory, through Calvary into Easter. The event
of the transfiguration of Christ on the Mount, which he had
discussed in one of his earliest books, is the source for our hope

that our personal suffering and the suffering of the cosmos will be transfigured by the power of the Spirit into the glory of God.

⋋ 35 ∾

The Glory of Self-Giving Love
From *Freedom, Faith, and the Future*, pp. 21-27.

Is God credible? I ask you to discuss one among the formidable considerations which cause some to say "no." The one which I choose is the suffering in the world. I do so for two reasons. One is that here the credibility of God is questioned with a special poignancy. The other is that here we face not only whether God is credible but what in the Christian sense it means for God to be God.

The problem is one which ethical monotheism has always had haunting its doorstep. It asserts that God is one, loving, and omnipotent, and meanwhile the world is a scene of appalling suffering. Which of us cannot be sensitive to the cries heard again and again in history: "Why has God allowed this?" "I may believe in God, but if I believe in him, how can I ever forgive him?" "It's God they ought to crucify instead of you and me."

We start by saying that a vast volume of human suffering is the result of human sinfulness and folly, the recurring unkindness of human beings to one another, an unkindness which has come to be entangled into the complex structures of the world's life. Human beings have misused their freedom and lent themselves and their powers to pride and greed and self-aggrandizement....It is this perversion of human life which theologians call the Fall; and the story of Adam and Eve in the Book of Genesis, incredible as an historical story, is a symbolic parable of the truth that human beings are free and responsible and have misused their freedom with catastrophic results. If it be asked whether the Creator could not make a good and happy world without these horrible possibilities, there is the answer that it is hard to see how there can be a moral universe, a universe in which ethics have meaning and love and virtue have existence, unless there is the free choice of the creature and the risks inherent in that.

Human beings choose to follow impulses of self-centeredness instead of the way of unselfishness, the way which is ultimately "die to live" to which conscience prompts them....The biblical writers summed up this state of affairs by saying that the world is "under judgment": a world whose actions bring calamity upon itself. To a world under judgment the biblical writers go on to say "repent," and repent means both "turn" and "be sorry." The share of any one of us in the total volume of the world's estrangement from God's goodness may seem to be infinitesimally small. But nothing is infinitesimally small in our relation to one who loves us and cares for us infinitely, and it is for each of us to repent—repent of that little area of the world's life for which he or she is responsible. Only thus, by putting myself right with God, am I likely to have the knowledge of him which can lead me to any understanding of this problem....

For the answer of faith we turn to the biblical writers. Their method is not to try to explain the problem or to explain it away, but somehow to carry it into the presence of God and to see what happens to it in that context....In sum their answer was this. Do not argue, do not theorize, keep near to God, in nearness to him things become different. "I will hold me fast by God." Keep near to him, and see what happens. That was the way of faith, and it is the way of faith still. "See what happens to you, and to the suffering, through God's nearness to you": it is a summons to a practical experience. But faith moves on to hope; and the people of faith in the Old Testament look forward, and they say; "Keep near to God. See what difference that makes. But also wait, God is going to act; look forward, God is going to do something." And the biblical writers use various kinds of imagery about what God is going to do: the imagery of the coming of the kingdom, the coming of the Messiah, the coming of the day of the Lord, the coming of God as deliverer.

What happened? The climax of the prophetic hope was the history of Jesus of Nazareth. Jesus came into Galilee as a prophet proclaiming that God's kingdom—that is, God's reign or sovereignty—is here. It was, he taught, present in the righteousness which he expounded, a righteousness embodied in himself. It was present, he also taught, in the acts of power which he performed. Many of those acts of power were directed to the removal of human suffering. Christians see in these works of healing by Jesus the authority and sanction for all time for Christians to strive to remove suffering in every way that they can, whether by prayer and sacrament or by medical science or by both. But if men and women looked to Jesus for a straightforward program of removing all suffering and substituting a painless world for a suffering world, they were disappointed; and they will be disappointed still. For at the heart of his message there is the call: repent, be sorry, turn to God and God's righteousness, become like little children in receiving his gifts of goodness. Suffering is hateful; men and women should be freed from it: but better learn righteousness and experience pain and sorrow than enjoy a painless world and continue in unrepenting selfishness.

We follow the story to its climax. So far from disappearing from the path of Jesus the forces of evil gathered strength, and it was clear that if he persisted in his mission those who hated his message and his claims would destroy him in death. But how did he view the death, terrible and ignominious, which lay in his path? Was it to be one more defeat of goodness, one more addition to the mountain of the problem of evil? No, it was to be, for Christianity, the secret of God's answer. Jesus taught the disciples, in the days before the final crisis, that though it would be wicked men who would perpetrate his death, it would be an event in which God's power, God's purpose, God's deliverance would be at work....

Jesus gave himself. He would not save himself. He gave himself to share in the deep darkness of a world sinful, estranged. But the apostles of Jesus came to believe that when Jesus died in this manner, giving himself and not saving himself, he was not contradicting the reign of God. Rather was he, the divine Son, showing what the reign of God is like and how the reign of God comes, indeed what God himself is like. In the utter self-giving of Jesus in the desolation of his death there is the divine self-giving love, the very essence of deity. So St. John, when he interprets the history in his own gospel, does not hesitate to describe the death as *glory*.

When Jesus dies we see the *glory* which is God's in all eternity, the glory of the self-giving love of the Triune God.

This is what Christianity, in its heart and its essence, is about.

Calvary was not a defeat which needed the resurrection to cancel it or avenge it or reverse it. No, Calvary was love's victory, God's power, God's reign. The resurrection came quickly to seal it, and to carry its effects onward into the subsequent centuries.

God is revealed in the event: the answer is given, the answer that in the suffering of the world God suffers, sharing, bearing, intimate with those who suffer if they will accept the intimacy which he offers them. There is a traditional doctrine that God is "impassible." Am I denying that doctrine? Essentially, I think not so. Is not the essential meaning of that old doctrine that God is perfect and supreme, and that his perfection can never be injured or reduced? God is never to be pitied, he is never thwarted or frustrated. If he suffers it is with a difference. He suffers not as one who is frustrated but in a suffering which flows from the love which is perfect and victorious. "I have overcome the world."

Where then does our faith stand? We believe indeed that God is omnipotent and sovereign. But his is always the sovereignty of a self-giving, pain-bearing love. There is no other sovereignty in the universe. In the imagery of the Apocalypse the Lamb (sacrificial self-giving) is on the throne (sovereignty). There is no throne except the throne where the Lamb is, the throne of Calvary. *There* we begin to see meaning, purpose, sovereignty within the world, *there* we begin to see the path which we can follow through the jungle of our frightening experiences. Where we see acts of sacrifice and love in human lives, these are not "lost" or wasted. They are the way to the heart of God himself, and they are used within his purpose of the overcoming of evil.

~ **36** ~

Does God Suffer?

From *An Era in Anglican Theology*, pp. 58-59.

Does God suffer? Traditional theology, patristic, scholastic, and reformed alike, has said that God is impassible. The question is too vast for us to discuss again here and now. But as we are sketching the history of Anglican teaching about the cross we have to notice the tendency, especially in the 1920s, to believe that the traditional doctrine of impassibility must be modified and that God suffers....

Theologically the most prominent teaching on this subject was in William Temple's *Christus Veritas*. It was teaching evoked no doubt by sensitivity to the distresses of the time, and congruous with the Hegelian strain in Temple's thought; but its root is in the plain theological insistence that Christ is the key to God as he eternally is, the cross is "the unveiling of a mystery of the Divine Life itself—the revelation of the cost whereby God wins victory over the evil which he had permitted" (p. 262). "All that we can suffer of physical or mental anguish is within the divine experience; he has known it all himself." There is a true sense in which God is "without passions," for he is never "passive" in the sense of having things happen to him except with his consent; but the traditional term really meant "incapable of suffering," and this Temple says is "almost wholly false." "Almost"! In that word there is on Temple's part a slight drawing back: and he seems to explain the "almost" by the sentence "It is truer to say that there is suffering in God than that God suffers." And why? "The suffering is an element in the joy of the triumphant sacrifice."

It is significant that while the argument, and in large measure the religious instinct, in *Christus Veritas* led Temple towards the assertion of divine suffering, there is yet this holding back. God suffers, not as one who is thwarted, but as one who wills to suffer in his purpose as supreme Creator and victorious Redeemer; and if we say that he suffers we may never pity him, for we are worshipers of him in a perfection beyond all our imagining. Equally characteristic of Anglican divinity have been both the move towards patripassianism and the drawing back: indeed, the double movement has sometimes been seen within the working of the mind of a single theologian. The first betokens the Christocentric strain in our theology: the drawing back betokens the sense of mystery and the sense of the adoration of the Creator in his perfection springing from our tradition of worship.

It may be possible to exaggerate, and yet it is wrong to belittle the extent of Baron von Hügel's influence in this regard: but the influence was there, and not least in the essay on "Suffering and God" which became well-known in Anglican circles through its inclusion in the second published series of *Essays and Addresses* (1926), the year after *Christus Veritas*. This essay goes deep into the implications of human creatureliness and God's perfection. No Anglican could easily write, as von Hügel wrote, of the divine "isness," or say that the "thirst of religion is, at bottom, a metaphysical thirst." Yet von Hügel influenced Anglicans so greatly because his teaching was congruous with that unity of theology and worship always latent in our tradition. The gratitude of the redeemed to their Redeemer for what he has done is interpenetrated by the creature's adoration of the Creator in the perfection of his Being.

∾ 37 ∾

The Mount and the Plain

From *Be Still and Know,* pp. 66-70.

Transfiguration is a central theme of Christianity, the transforming of sufferings and circumstances, of men and women with the vision of Christ before them and the Holy Spirit within them. The language both of vision and of transformation is found in the Pauline, Johannine, and Petrine writings in the New Testament, and the language tells of Christian experience which recurs through the centuries. This is not to say that there are many conscious references to the transfiguration story in the New Testament writings, but only that the themes are recurring Christian themes and the transfiguration is a symbol of them.

The transfiguring of suffering is attested in Christian life. Sometimes a person suffers greatly, and the suffering continues and does not disappear; but through nearness to Christ there is seen a courage, an outgoing love and sympathy, a power of prayer, a Christlikeness of a wonderful kind. It is a privilege of the Christian pastor to be meeting these experiences and to be learning from them more than he or she can ever teach. In the testimony to these experiences in the apostolic writings perhaps the most moving instance is near the end of chapter eight of the letter to the Romans.

> Who shall separate us from the love of Christ? Shall tribulation, or distress, or persecution, or famine, or nakedness, or peril, or sword?...No, in all these things we are more than conquerors through him who loved us. (Rom. 8:35, 37)

I love the comment of Karl Barth on the passage:

> Thus our tribulation, without ceasing to be tribulation, is transformed. We suffer as we suffered before, but our suffering is no longer a passive perplexity, but is transformed into a pain which is creative, fruitful, full of power and promise. The road which is impassable has been made known to us in the crucified and risen Lord.

Circumstances are transfigured. Something blocks your path, some fact of life or person or obstacle which is utterly thwarting and frustrating. It seems impossible to remove it or ignore it or surmount it. But when it is seen in a larger context, and that context is Jesus crucified and risen, it is in a new orbit of relationships and while it remains, it remains differently. A phrase of St. Paul in 2 Corinthians 4 seems to interpret the experience, when he contrasts our "light affliction" with the "exceeding weight of glory," the one belonging to time and the other to eternity. Such is the transforming of circumstances, not by their abolition but by the lifting of them into the orbit of a crucified and risen Jesus.

Central indeed is the theme of the transforming of persons. Several passages in the apostolic writings describe this in relation to the vision of Christ as the goal and the power of the Spirit within. It is too much to say that there is a conscious reference to the event of the transfiguration but it can indeed be said that the symbolism of the event is linked with the characteristics of the Christian life. In 2 Corinthians 3 St. Paul is using allegorical imagery to contrast the old covenant of the time of Moses and the new covenant in the gospel. The first brought condemnation, the second brings liberty. The first is linked with the passing radiance on the face of Moses, the second with an enduring light of glory which Christians are able both to see and to reflect.

> We all, with unveiled face, beholding the glory of the Lord, are being changed into his likeness from one degree of glory to another; for this comes from the Lord who is the Spirit. (2 Cor. 3:18)

Christians gaze, not indeed directly but as in a glass or mirror, upon the glory of God, for Jesus is its perfect mirror and reflection. With this vision before them they are changed into his likeness, and it is the Holy Spirit who as Lord works the change within them.

Another passage about the transforming of Christians mentions neither the vision nor the indwelling Spirit but probes deeply into the way in which the transforming happens.

> I appeal to you therefore, brethren, by the mercies of God, to present your bodies as a living sacrifice, holy and acceptable to God, which is your spiritual worship. Do not be conformed to this world but be transformed by the renewal of your mind, that you may prove what is the will of God, what is good and acceptable and perfect. (Rom. 12:1-2)

It all begins by God's own *mercy*. Responding to that mercy the apostle bids his fellow Christians offer their own lives as a *sacrifice*, for that is the true meaning of worship. Then there must come a radical *break with the world*; conformity to its ways and ideas must be abandoned. Refusing the conformity to the world we can then be *transformed* towards Christ, and the secret of this transforming is to be given a *new mind*, and that mind is no doubt the mind of

Christ, vividly portrayed in Philippians 2 as the mind of the one who became a servant. Through the transforming and the receiving of a new mind it becomes possible to discern what is the *will of God* and what are those things describable as good and perfect. Here indeed is a searching analysis of the transforming of human lives.

In these ways the transfiguring of suffering, circumstances, and people belongs to the experience of the Christian life as well as to the apostolic teaching. But the teaching looks forward also to a transfiguring in the future. St. Paul in Colossians tells of how the present life of the Christians in union with the risen life of Jesus will have fulfillment at the coming of Christ: "When Christ who is our life appears, then you also will appear with him in glory" (Col. 3:4). The first epistle of John tells of the present sonship of Christians finding fulfillment in a day when their likeness to Jesus and vision of God will be realized:

> Beloved, we are God's children now; it does not yet appear what we shall be, but we know that when he appears we shall be like him, for we shall see him as he is. (1 John 3:2)

Here indeed is the fulfillment of the Lord's promise, "Blessed are the pure in heart, for they shall see God."

Be still and know. The scene on the mount speaks to us today, but we are not allowed to linger there. We are bidden to journey on to Calvary and there to learn of the darkness and the desolation which are the cost of the glory. But from Calvary and Easter there comes a Christian hope of immense range: the hope of the transformation not only of humankind but of the cosmos too. In Eastern Christianity especially there has been the continuing belief that Easter is the beginning of a transformed cosmos. There is indeed a glimpse of this hope in St. Paul's letter to the Romans, a hope that "the creation itself will be set free from its bondage to decay and obtain the glorious liberty of the children of God." The bringing of humankind to glory will be the prelude to the beginning of all creation. Is this hope mere fantasy? At its root there is the belief in the divine sovereignty of sacrificial love, a sovereignty made credible only by transfigured lives.

~: 38 ~

The Gospel of Transfiguration

From *The Glory of God and the Transfiguration of Christ,* pp. 144-147.

The transfiguration does not belong to the central core of the gospel. The apostolic *Kerygma* did not, so far as we know, include it; and it would be hard for Christians to claim that the salvation of humankind could not be wrought without it. But it stands as a gateway to the saving events of the gospel, and is as a mirror in which the Christian mystery is seen in its unity. Here we perceive that the living and the dead are one in Christ, that the old covenant and the new are inseparable, that the cross and the glory are of one, that the age to come is already here, that our human nature has a destiny of glory, that in Christ the final word is uttered and in him alone the Father is well-pleased. Here the diverse elements in the theology of the New Testament meet.

Forgetfulness of the truths for which the transfiguration stands has often led to distortions. The severance of the New Testament from the Old, the cleavage between God the Redeemer and God the Creator are obvious illustrations. It is possible, alike in Christology and in sacramental teaching and in the idea of the Christian life, to regard the supernatural as replacing the natural in such a way as to "overthrow the nature of a sacrament." It is possible to regard the redemptive act of God in Christ in terms so transcendental that nature and history are not seen in real relation to it, or to identify the divine act with nature and history in such a way that the other-worldly tension of the gospel is forgotten. Against these distortions the transfiguration casts its light in protest.

"The transfiguration," wrote F. D. Maurice, "has lived on through ages, and shed its light upon all ages....In the light of that countenance which was altered, of that raiment which was white and glistering, all human countenances have acquired a brightness, all common things have been transfigured."[1] So great is the impact of theology upon language that the word "transfigure," drawn from a biblical story to which scant attention has often been paid, has entered into the practical vocabulary of the Christian life.

To Christians suffering is transfigured. Karl Barth wrote:

> Our tribulation, without ceasing to be tribulation, is transformed. We must suffer, as we suffered before, but our suffering is no longer a passive perplexity... but is transformed into a pain which is fruitful, creative, full of power and promise.... The road which is impassable has been made known to us in the crucified and risen Lord.[2]

To Christians knowledge is transfigured. The knowledge of the world and its forces may be used for the service of human pride and human destruction, or else for the unfolding of God's truth and the enlarging of God's worship. Dr. Hort wrote:

> It is not too much to say that the gospel itself can never be fully known till nature as well as man is fully known; and that the manifestation of nature as well as man in Christ is part of his manifestation of God. As the gospel is the perfect introduction to all truth, so on the other hand it is in itself known only in proportion as it is used for the enlightenment of departments of truth which seem at first sight to lie beyond its boundaries.... The earth as well as the heaven is full of God's glory, and his visible glory is but the garment of his truth, so that every addition to truth becomes a fresh opportunity for adoration.[3]

To Christians the world is transfigured. Liberated from its dominance they discover it afresh as the scene both of divine judgment and of divine renewal within the new creation of Christ. The measure in which they accept the judgment is the measure in which they discern, in the face of every calamity, the divine renewal in the raising of the dead.

The transfiguring of pain, of knowledge, and of the world is attested in centuries of the experience of Christians. It comes neither by an acceptance of things as they are nor by a flight from

---

1. *The Gospel of the Kingdom of Heaven*, p. 157.
2. *The Epistle to the Romans*, p. 156.
3. F. J. A. Hort, *The Way, The Truth, The Life*, pp. 83-84.

them, but by that uniquely Christian attitude which the story of the transfiguration represents. It is an attitude which is rooted in detachment—for pain is hateful, knowledge is corrupted, and the world lies in the evil one—but which so practices detachment as to return and perceive the divine sovereignty in the very things from which the detachment has had to be. Thus the Christian life is a rhythm of going and coming; and the gospel narrative of the ascent of Hermon, the metamorphosis and the descent to a faithless and perverse generation is a symbol of the mission of the church in its relation to the world....

Confronted as they are with a universe more than ever terrible in the blindness of its processes and the destructiveness of its potentialities, human beings must be led to the Christian faith not as a panacea of progress nor as an other-worldly solution unrelated to history, but as a gospel of transfiguration. Such a gospel both transcends the world and speaks to the immediate here-and-now. He who is transfigured is the Son of Man; and, as he discloses on mount Hermon another world, he reveals that no part of created things and no moment of created time lies outside the power of the Spirit, who is Lord, to change from glory to glory.

IX

THE MYSTICAL BODY
OF CHRIST

Bishop Ramsey wrote much about the church, as was appropriate for one who was by his position so much involved with its affairs. The following writing will show, however, that he was little concerned with the perquisites and powers of the institution. His thinking always dwelt upon the relationship of the church to Christ and the work of the church through the power of the Holy Spirit. Once again, cross and resurrection dominate his reflections upon the church, and how that event at the center of the gospel must govern how we understand and believe in the church.

He also wrote much about the eucharist as the liturgical action through which men and women are united with Christ through the worship of the church. Indeed, it was this vision of the church as a eucharistic community that lay behind all of this efforts toward the unity of the church. The hope for unity must always be focused, he believed, upon the truth and holiness of God. Such a unity is only possible for the scattered Body of Christ through prayer and the carrying out of God's purpose in the world.

～ **39** ～

The Church's Origin

From *The Resurrection of Christ*, pp. 96-101.

The exalted Christ is incomplete without the church. It is through the church that he lives and works. The essence of the church is not the members who belong to it but the Christ from whom its life is derived. It is he, and not they, that provides the church's definition.

But the foundation of the church upon the resurrection implies for it a constant relation to the passion also. It is by baptism into the death of Christ that we are made his members, and it is by a continually renewed relation to his death that our membership is sustained.

The New Testament shows how the Christian life thus began and thus continued. The convert reaches out by faith from herself to Christ who died for her, renouncing the life-unto-self. She plunges beneath the waters of baptism as one who dies, and she emerges into a new life in Christ who rose again. "Are ye ignorant, that all we who were baptized into Christ Jesus were baptized into his death?" (Rom. 6:3). But the convert's relation to the cross does not cease there. The living Christ, to whom she now belongs, is still Christ the Crucified One; and the Christian advances in "the fellowship of his sufferings, being conformed unto his death" (Phil. 3:21). If once for all she has "died with Christ" (Col. 3:3), she is not exempt from the subsequent command, "Mortify therefore your members which are upon the earth" (Col. 3:5). The convert is ever near to the cross in her own conflict with sin; in her bearing of sorrow, pain, and humiliation when they come to her; in her bearing of the pain of others; in her increasing knowledge of what Calvary meant and means. But in all this she is discovering that the risen life of Jesus belongs to her, and with it great rejoicing. Awhile perhaps it may be that the cross is more apparent to her, and the risen life may seem to be hidden. But one day the secret that is already present will be made manifest, and in the resurrection that awaits her after death she will see the risen Christ in whose life, though hidden, she has already shared.

Cross and resurrection are the ground of the church's origin, the secret of the church's contemporary being, the goal of the church's final self-realization on behalf of the human race. The word and the sacraments in the midst of the church make known to its members continually what is their origin, their secret and their goal. For the *word* is the word of the cross, whereby the church is made, renewed, and judged. The *eucharist* is the proclaiming of the Lord's death until his coming again; the setting forth before God and his people of the whole drama of his life, death, resurrection, and parousia; and the feeding of his people with his broken body and outpoured blood. The eucharist looks back to the events of the gospel; it realizes those events in the present hour; it anticipates the final consummation: "the Body of our Lord Jesus Christ which was given for thee preserve thy body and soul unto everlasting life."...

It is, however, not only in the New Testament that the biblical meaning of the church is disclosed. For just as the resurrection sent the apostles back to the Old Testament in their understanding of Jesus Christ, so it sends us back to the Old Testament to find there some permanent truths about the church in its relation to God and to the world....

The church of Israel was called by God not to glorify itself but to make him known to the nation. It possessed an imperishability, not on account of any merits of its members but on account of the faithfulness of God who wills to use Israel for the redemption of humankind. When Israel fails, the judgment of God falls and punishment follows: yet there is a remnant whom God uses as the stump from which a new and better tree may grow. God does not find the Israelites of any particular generation to be indispensable: he is not pledged to them, if they are unfaithful to him; he can sweep them aside, and from the stones of a heathen world he can raise up new ones who will serve him better. But Israel continues imperishable, even if its true mission be represented by a very small number or by the lonely Christ, who bears the destiny of Israel to Calvary and to the grave.

For the God of Israel is the God who judges and raises up. His people come to learn of him and to make him known not by the even tenor of a steady spiritual growth, but through crises of judgment and resurrection. Great deliverances and times of spiritual prosperity are followed by the disasters born of pride and complacency: humiliation follows, and in the day of humiliation God raises up his servants and prophets. What is true of the old Israel is true also of the new. Centuries of achievement lead on to stagnation and self-sufficiency, and the God who raised up Moses, Amos, Jeremiah, Ezra raises up Benedict, Francis, Wesley, Keble. The church is judged when it gives the glory to itself: it is renewed only by accepting the judgment and by being raised again to seek the glory of God in the service of men and women.

But if the comparison between the old Israel and the new is important, it is no less important to notice where the contrast lies. It lies most chiefly in the fact that whereas the old Israel was sustained by repeated actions of God in raising her up, the new Israel has behind it and within it the one, final, decisive passion and resurrection of Christ. Her mission is to make his passion and resurrection known, so that humankind may learn in the midst of every historical crisis both the judgment and the mercy which the passion and resurrection bring. And she fulfills her mission only by being brought herself again and again beneath that judgment and mercy which she teaches to humankind.

◡⋮ 40 ⋮◠

On the Apostolic Church

From *The Gospel and the Catholic Church*, pp. 140ff.

The importance of the age of the Fathers must not be misunderstood. It is important, not as a golden age nor as a model for the imitation of Christians (as the Tractarians somewhat extravagantly claimed), but as an age when the whole gospel found expression in the life and liturgy of the one Body, with a balanced use of all the church's structure and with a depth and breadth and unity which contrast strikingly with every subsequent epoch. In these early centuries the Syrian, the Greek, and the Roman were in one fellowship, with a eucharistic worship exhibiting something like a balance of all the elements of thanksgiving, commemoration, fellowship, sacrifice, mystery. The church was world-renouncing, first with its martyrs and later with its hermits, and also world-redeeming, with its baptism of Greek culture and humanism into the Faith. Amid all these varieties of type and of temper the Body was one; and the doctrine of the mystical Body retained its inner depth and breadth since the doctrine of redemption still controlled it.

The close relation between the doctrines of the Body and of redemption is apparent in all the important teaching about the church from St. Paul to St. Augustine. But at an early date there appear differences of emphasis between the East and the West.

The Greek Fathers

There is little variety in the teaching of the Eastern theologians about the mystical Body. They thought and wrote mainly of its place in God's purpose of uniting humankind in Christ, and more of its inner relation to the incarnation than of its outward order and the practical problems concerning it....

That Greek Catholicism had its dangers is undeniable, but it bears striking witness to certain elements of Christianity which are less apparent in Latin and in modern church-life and doctrine. Firstly, it is noteworthy that the Greek Fathers gave their deepest teaching about the church without treating the church as a separate subject in itself. They did not expound the church; they expounded Christ the Redeemer, and in such a way that the church was included in their exposition. And indeed the glory of the church is most apparent not when it is buttressed and defended as an institution but when, without any particular "church-consciousness," it is seen as the spontaneous glory of the Christ.

Secondly, the Greek phrase *soma Christou* in itself speaks a truth which every translation tends to obscure. The church is not a "corpus" in the sense of a corporation or institution, somewhat external to its members. It is an organism whose members are one with Christ who is its essence. With this truth enshrined in their language and with a certain avoidance of western legalism, the Greeks were able to keep their thought about the one Body more free from the "externalizing" and "institutionalizing" tendency. Hence the Easterns have insisted that the word "catholic" describes not only external universality, reaching to every race and land, but also internal wholeness, whereby every member has his or her share in *to kath holou*. Church life and the life of the soul are identical.

Thirdly—and this springs from the previous facts—the cultus of the saints in the East is practiced as a part of the life of the one Body. It does not mean the elevation of marked individuals to special places of influence and intercessory power, enthroned between God and us. It means rather the giving glory to Christ in his one Body, whose family life (in the seen and in the unseen) is a manifestation of Christ's own life. Hence, in the East, there has never been the rigid distinction apparent in the West between "praying to" and "praying for" the saints and the departed; the sense of the one family prevents such rigid conceptions and binds saints and sinners in one, for the sainthood belongs only to the one Body which is Holy. In reverencing a saint the people reverence the life of Christ who is the life of them all. Hence also the eastern cultus of the Virgin Mary, the Mother of God, has meant the veneration not of an isolated figure enthroned in heaven but of one who is humanity indwelt by God, herself the first-fruits of the church, in whom is focused uniquely in history the truth about the whole Body of Christ....

Fourthly, the ideas of truth and authority in the East have been more free from the legalistic and scholastic tendencies apparent in the West. Truth and tradition reside in the Body as a whole; they are not something clerically imposed upon the Body. Hence truth is very close to life and worship. Both in Russian and in Slavonic the phrase *he orthodoxia* is translated so as to mean not right "opinion" but right "glory" or "worship." Hence while the danger of intellectual stagnation and of superstition is ever present, doctrine is always related to the Body's whole life. The singing of the creed in the liturgy is introduced by the words, "Let us love one another, that with one accord we may confess...."

Indeed the deepest initiation into Eastern Orthodoxy comes not from the texts of the Fathers but from sharing in the liturgy. For there the worshiper will find what the textbook can never make articulate, the sense (as prominent in the East as that of the crucifixion is prominent in the West) of the triumph of Christ who has risen from the dead, and has shattered the gates of hell, of the resurrection as the present fact about the Christians who are his Body, of the heavenly host whose praises are shared by the family on earth.

The Western Fathers

While the Greek Fathers dwelt upon the church's inner relation with the incarnation, the Latin Fathers were more concerned with thinking out its relation with the men and women from whom it was composed, and with tackling the practical problems of grace and freedom, of sin and guilt, and of church order. At an early date a legalistic temper is apparent in Latin theology; the Latin mind naturally inclined towards this temper; the great influence of Tertullian accentuated it, and the particular problems faced by the western church gave scope for its exercise. The brunt of the conflict caused by the first schisms was borne by the western church. Both Novatianism and Donatism were schismatic movements expressing an extreme puritanical tendency, and insisting that those who had once apostatized under persecution could not be readmitted to Christian fellowship. Both movements claimed to be themselves alone the true church. And in face of problems such as these, the western theologians, instead of resting in the contemplation of the church's inner mystery, were compelled to tackle the question, who are in the church and who are not?...

A certain rigidity is apparent [in Cyprian's thinking]. Novationist baptisms and orders are invalid, says St. Cyprian. The contemporary church in Rome would not follow St. Cyprian in this attitude, and the less rigid view in the end prevailed as regards baptisms and orders. How, then, are we to estimate St. Cyprian's own view? Firstly, it springs at bottom not from legalism, but from a sense of the church as the indivisible home of love. The church *cannot* be divided; there can be but one church, inward and outward, and the only sacraments are those which are acts of this one church. This sense that a divided church is a monstrous impossibility is indeed the needful basis of all Christian thinking about the church.

Secondly, while the episcopate is essential, along with the scriptures and sacraments, to the church's one and complete life, it may be asked whether it is legitimate to treat the episcopate as *in itself* the ground and the test of church unity. There is in Cyprian an attempt to base unity upon episcopacy as the one and outstanding bond. But episcopacy cannot bear alone the whole weight of the tensions of controversy; and the pure Cyprianic theory seems to break when St. Cyprian himself is found in an impasse with his brother bishop, Stephen of Rome.

Thirdly, while St. Cyprian's denial of the baptism and the orders of schismatics was rejected later in favor of St. Augustine's "wider" view, it was linked with a deeply Catholic sense of the church which the later view may often miss. To St. Cyprian validity of orders depended upon their derivation from and their exercise within the one life of the whole church. The first fact must be the church's corporate family life; then come valid orders which are an organ of that whole life. The later view was "broader"; it recognized the orders of the schismatics, but it opened the way towards the view that valid orders come first, perhaps even as an isolated channel of grace, and that church life depends solely upon them. A return to the Cyprianic view would enable clearer and more Catholic thinking about the meaning of a valid ministry in a reunited church.

St. Augustine was confronted with the menace of the Donatist schism, and he faced it with teaching handed down from St. Cyprian, which he now modified and expanded in certain ways. His doctrine of the church left a deep impact upon the whole subsequent history of the church, and indeed upon the history of European politics. It is a teaching as complex as is any part of his many-sided life and character as bishop, doctor, and mystic....

The underlying conviction of St. Augustine was that truth and charity exist only in the one Catholic Body. The sacraments belonged to that Body. Yet God was the author and the agent in them, hence baptism into the Name was real baptism wherever performed. And in his longing for peace St. Augustine abandoned the rigid and Cyprianic view that baptism and orders are invalid outside the church. By delicately and reverently challenging the authority of the greatest African doctor then known he insisted that baptism and ordination are valid wherever carried out. Their full effect could only be realized by restoration into the one church; nonetheless the rites were real rites, God being their agent, and neither rebaptism nor reordination was necessary. Amid all the variety of thought and statement, which makes single quotations from the anti-Donatist letters so meaningless, this practical policy emerges as St. Augustine's own contribution. He urged the laxer view, and the laxer view prevailed.

But if this new view was "broader," it contained the seeds of much perversity in later history. For while the Cyprianic view makes orders utterly dependent upon the church and validity a part of the church's single life in grace, the Augustinian view leaves room for thinking of orders as valid apart from the church's corporate life and for the idea of succession by orders as a single and isolated channel of grace. St. Augustine has "broadened" church theory; but he has opened the way for a line of thought which glories in the name of Catholic but which severs the doctrine of orders from the doctrine of the Body of Christ....

The depth and the complexity of St. Augustine's teaching make him a figure in history which defies analysis. Indeed, he himself defied the claims of consistency. Into him there flow many of the currents of thought and experience within and without the church of the Fathers. And from him there have been deduced theories which, when isolated from his other teaching, have destroyed the balance of Catholic truth. He stands thus on the brink of the division between Catholicism and its later perversions. Isolate his statements about the validity of orders apart from the life of the church, and there is the "clericalist" view of apostolic succession. Isolate his lapse into persecution and his language about the kingdom of God on earth, and there is a basis for the medieval church-theocracy. Isolate his teaching about grace and sin and predestination, and there is the cruder element in the theology of the Reformation. Such is the complexity of St. Augustine, himself a creative chapter in the history of humankind.

St. Augustine thus appears to the historian as the creative religious genius molding the movement of some of the greatest forces in human life and thought. But he was creative because he had himself been created by Christ in his church. He became what he became through the Christ who converted him and through the one Body in which he learned and prayed, and, in the Pauline sense, died and lived. In him was focused in full measure the life of the church of God, in all its rich variety.

And the church of the Fathers had a unity and a life which was one. For all the differences between the East, with it mysticism, its conservatism, its concern with the church's inner relation to the incarnation, its liturgical emphasis upon the resurrection, and the West, with its practical bent, its concern with problems of order, its sense of personal guilt, its tendency towards legalism—it is still true to speak of the one church of the Fathers. For the balanced doctrine of *unum corpus, hen soma* is taught, and this doctrine is dominated by the doctrine of redemption.

The structure of scripture, creed, episcopate, sacraments is still intact as one whole; no element in this structure fails to have its due attention. If the See of Rome is advancing in prestige and beginning to press its claims unduly, the sense of the episcopate as the organ of unity is still powerful. If the idea of an isolated clerical priesthood is threatening, there is still the teaching of an Augustine and a Chrysostom about the truly eucharistic meaning of the *Corpus Christi* or *soma Christou*. If the dogmatic debates are sometimes tedious, the theme which dominates them is still the redemptive work of Christ. If there is talk of an earthly kingdom which is the church, there is still the New Testament sense of the "not yet" and of the *ecclesia qualis tunc erit*. There is, in other words, a doctrine of the mystical Body with its Pauline and its Johannine features still manifest. The phrase *to kath holou* has a meaning for the centuries between St. Paul and the fall of the Western Empire. The study of the gospel in the New Testament forces us to study the church of the Fathers; the church of the Fathers still shows us Christ crucified and risen, and a Body which is one.

↲   **41**   ↳

What is the Church?

A sermon preached on the eve of St. Peter's Day in 1972
in Lincoln Cathedral; from *Canterbury Pilgrim*, pp. 82-86.

Today at St. Peter's festival, let St. Peter himself tell us the deepest meaning of Lincoln Cathedral. Every Christian church was built because there exists this other church of which St. Peter tells. Listen to his words: "Come to Jesus, to that living stone...like living stones be yourselves built up a spiritual house" (1 Peter 2:4-5). That is what the word "church" meant to the Christians of the first century: not stone or brick or wood, but the Christian people themselves. Jesus rejected by men and done to death on Calvary but precious in God's sight and now raised from the dead, is the cornerstone; and when people are converted and baptized they are united to him, and there grows, stone by stone, stone by stone, a spiritual house, Christ's home, Christ's temple, through whom Christ is now made known in the world. It is of this house of God that this cathedral is a symbol; and of all its glories the greatest is that it is a symbol of the house made of human lives. Through the centuries this other great church and minster has stood: human lives united to Jesus, receiving his presence, and showing his goodness, his love, his sacrifice, his humility, his compassion. Living stones, what a mingling of metaphors! It tells of firm, solid, unmovable loyalty, and of persons alive in joy, in freedom, in creativity, in influence. This is the church which Jesus Christ founded, the church of which he said that the gates of death would never prevail against it.

Some searching questions are posed for all of us today. We think of the Christians of the first century. They met in one another's houses to pray together, to celebrate the eucharist, to listen to the letters from an apostle, to practice fellowship in every way. Or sometimes they met in the open air, near to some river or stream in which the converts were baptized. *They* were God's house, and they knew no other. The great cathedrals were not yet. We can think too of how today there are Christians in countries of great poverty who have the simplest churches built of wood or mud, and they love them dearly and walk many miles to worship in them. Or we can think too of countries today where Christians are severely persecuted, and it is the homes of the people once again that are the meeting places of the believers. In all these ways Christians have shown, and Christians show still, that it is the people, not the buildings, that make the church of God. There are places in this country, not least in new areas of population, where this is most strikingly so.

What thoughts rise in our minds as we remember these facts?

Firstly, we need not apologize or regret that when Christianity moved into the world's civilizations and cultures in order to try to bring Christ's Spirit within them, there followed the baptism of painting and music and letters and architecture into the service and praise of God, men and women offering to God the greatest beauty that they have to offer. Human works, as well as human beings themselves, are claimed by God and brought to him. Hence the story of Christian art, sculpture, and architecture through the centuries, never with the Godward motive absent but always with that risk of mingled motives that belongs to our fallible nature.

Next, we must realize how possible it is amid the complexities of Christian civilization to miss the simple truth of St. Peter's teaching that the church means essentially the people themselves as living stones. Not seldom have people been led to suppose that the church means the buildings, that their upkeep is one of the primary Christian functions. Indeed, Christianity can itself appear to be identified with a particular sort of western European culture with its chancels and naves and organs and pews and hassocks. Hence it is not surprising that, in reaction, forms of Christian fellowship are today springing up apart from the historic institutional churches, with Christians meeting in houses to worship and pray together, to study the Bible together, to break the bread together, feeling after the mood and the atmosphere of the first Christians. "Experimental Christianity" as it is sometimes called, in contrast to institutional Christianity, may prove to be a growing phenomenon in our time. Indeed, it may be that the ecumenical task of the future will be less the holding together of the various older traditions, Catholic, Anglican, Protestant, than the holding together of the old institutional churches on the one hand and the experimental types of Christianity on the other. What is certain is that exciting days for Christianity lie ahead.

Thirdly, St. Peter's words challenge us about our own priorities as a Christian church. What are the priorities in our hearts? I chanced the other day to read these words in John Ruskin's *Lectures on Art:*

> ...so, from day to day and from strength to strength you shall build up, by Art, by Thought and by Just Will, an *ecclesia* of England of which it shall not be said "See what manner of stones are here" but "See what manner of men."

"See what manner of men." Ruskin so rightly and characteristically saw how glorious architecture has its counterpart in lovely human lives. Perhaps a little naively he believed that art and letters sufficed of themselves to create Christian character, to build a Christian community. St. Peter knew better. He knew about the deep estrangement of human sin. He knew, as he tells us in his First Epistle, that little gem among the books of the New Testament, how Christ bore our sins in his own body on the tree, that we being dead to sin might live to righteousness, and how it was God who begat us again to a living hope by the resurrection of Jesus Christ from the dead. He knew that such alone is the foundation of the true community of a spiritual house. Jesus is the cornerstone, as being also the stone rejected in his passion and restored in his resurrection.

See what manner of stones are here, in this lovely Minster of Lincoln. See too what manner of men and women. May we before we go home today picture to ourselves what Christ's spiritual house might be, fulfilling the dreams of the old missionaries of this land. I see a community of Christians conscious of being called apart in the way of holiness, but never self-conscious as their awareness is of the God whom they worship and the people whom they serve and care for. I see such a community ardently devoted to the worship of God in a worship where awe and beauty and mystery are mingled with homeliness and fellowship. I see such a community practicing fellowship among themselves as the walls of denominations yield to the discovery of unity in Christ's truth. I see such a community marked by an intellectual integrity, open both to old truth and to new discovery, a thoughtful faith which is, in St. Peter's words, "always ready to give an answer to any man who asks a reason concerning the hope that is in you." I see such a community full of active compassion for the poor, the homeless, the hungry, the lonely. Such a community will influence the country as a whole with the ideals of service not to the group or the section but to the common good, ideals reacting far beyond our own country. Such a community will make Christ known because its members are living stones, Christ's own house in beauty and in lively steadfastness.

꒦ 42 ꒪

The Praise of His Glory

From *The Glory of God and the Transfiguration of Christ*, pp. 98-99.

At the heart of the church's glorifying of God there is the new rite of the eucharist. Here the church is united to the glory of Christ on Calvary and in heaven, and finds the focus of the glorifying of God by all created things.

In the upper room our Lord gave thanks to God over the loaf at the beginning of the supper and over the cup at the end of the supper; identified the loaf with his body and the wine with his blood—that is, with his life surrendered in sacrificial offering; bade his disciples partake of both the body and the blood; predicted a feasting with them in the messianic age. This eucharistic action may be interpreted by the language of the Fourth Gospel. Inasmuch as our Lord, by his actions and words with the loaf and the cup, is declaring himself to be dedicated to a sacrificial death, he is indeed glorifying the Father (John 17:1) and consecrating himself on behalf of the disciples (John 17:19). Inasmuch as he bids the disciples to feed upon his life surrendered as a sacrifice it is here that "the glory which thou gavest me I have given unto them" (John 17:22). The food which they receive is the life of Christ laid down in Godward offering: the glory which they are given is the glory wherewith Christ glorified the Father.

Thus the subsequent eucharistic worship of the church is on its Godward side a participation in Christ's glorifying of the Father, and on its humanward side a receiving of Christ's glory—the glory of the cross. Inasmuch as the rite is a showing-forth of Christ's death (1 Cor. 11:26) it recalls the glory of Calvary. Inasmuch as it is a sharing in the body of Christ and in the blood of Christ (1 Cor. 10:16) it unites those who partake with the glory of Christ as he now is—risen, ascended, and glorifying the Father. Inasmuch as it employs God's common gifts of bread and wine and brings them to be blessed, it is a glorifying of the Creator by the giving back of his own created gifts to him. And inasmuch as it points forward to the coming of Christ again (1 Cor. 11:26) it is an anticipation of that feasting with Christ in the world to come, when him whom we now perceive by faith we shall behold with open face.

Inasmuch as the glory is the glory of Father and Son in the bond of love, the eucharistic gift of glory to the disciples is tested in their unity. The Pauline "we being many are one bread, one body, for we all partake of the one bread" is tested in the Johannine "the glory which thou hast given me I have given unto them; that they may be one, even as we are one" (John 17:22). The new covenant in the blood of Christ is inseparable from the new commandment of mutual love in the manifestation of Christ's own love (John 13:31-35). Hence the common life of the Christian fellowship is not only a witness to the glory, but is itself the glory of the Father and the Son shown forth to the world. Without this common life, *ichabod*, the glory is departed.

⤳ 43 ⤳

Unity, Holiness, and Truth

An address to the Assembly of the World Council
of Churches in New Delhi, November 1961;
from *Canterbury Essays and Addresses*, pp. 55-57.

Today as we Christian people from every part of the world and from many different traditions meet in New Delhi to work for unity, the supreme fact, towering above all else, is the unceasing intercession of our Lord. The seventeenth chapter of the Gospel of St. John is the utterance, amid the historical crisis of the world's salvation, of a prayer which is everlasting. Our Great High Priest is interceding. And for what does he pray? That his disciples may be one, that they may be sanctified, that they may be sanctified in truth. Unity, holiness, truth; as the prayer is indivisible, so the fulfillment is indivisible too. It is useless to think that we can look for unity in Christ's name unless we are looking no less for holiness in his obedience and for the realization of the truth which he has revealed.

The words of the prayer tell, however, not only of aspirations for the future, but of gifts, once for all given to the church. By his presence in the Body of which he is the head, he has given to us already unity in himself and in the Father; he has given to us the holiness whose essence is his own self-consecration to his death upon the cross; and he has given to us the truth which is himself, the very truth incarnate. But it is in the earthen vessels of our frailty that these gifts are ours. Never has there been a moment when the church has not possessed the gifts, never a moment—since the friction in Jerusalem about widows or in Antioch about eating together or in Corinth about partisanship—when the church has not obscured the gifts by the sinfulness of its members. In fulfilling its mission the church has involved itself in the world's life, for its members have always their double citizenship of heaven and earth, their double standing as the redeemed and members of earthly communities.

Hence the church must live out its unity among the changing pressures of culture and polity; it must realize its holiness amid the complexities of successive civilizations; and it must learn and teach its truth amid varieties of intellectual system and method. Small wonder then that amid this involvement truth in the church has been obscured by human sophistications, holiness has been compromised by worldly pressure, unity has been torn by these causes and many more. All the while the church shows Christ to the world (for so great is his mercy that he uses the church mightily despite the failure of its members), and all the while the church tragically obscures him. But let us get our diagnosis right. Just as our mission is unity, holiness, truth, all three, so our scandal is the distortion of unity, holiness, truth, all three. No less is it in respect of all three that the call comes to our penitence, and our prayer for cleansing and renewal.

The world does not hear the call to holiness, and does not care for the truth in Christ. But the world has its own care for unity, albeit conceived in a secular way; longing for peace it desires that peoples and nations shall be joined to each other and the forces which separate them removed. And the world, caring thus for unity, is shocked when the church fails to manifest it. Yet while the world's criticism might rightly humble us, we must not on that account accept the world's conception of the matter. It is not just unity, togetherness with one another, that we seek; and ecclesiastics have sometimes slipped into talking as if it were, isolating unity from the other notes of the church. It is for unity in truth and holiness that we work and pray, for that is Christ's supernatural gift to us. Let that always be made clear. A movement which concentrates on unity as an isolated concept can mislead the world and mislead us, as indeed would a movement which had the exclusive label of holiness or the exclusive label of truth.

It is when we get back to the depth and comprehensiveness of our Lord's prayer that we see the depth and comprehensiveness of our quest for unity. What does it include? It includes the ascetical, as well as the intellectual and the diplomatic and ethical. It includes the negotiation of the union of churches, and of the bringing of churches into practical fellowship. It includes the task, with them all, of learning the truth in Christ, in scripture, in the Fathers, in the liturgies, in contemporary scholarship, in the self-criticism of systems and formulations, a task in which we have been finding ourselves, thank God, rather less like rivals and rather more like fellow-learners. It includes the doing by all of us, and where possible together, of those things which belong to our under-standing of Christian conscience, so that even now Christendom may be a reality with an impact and a voice. It includes the ministering to Christ in those who are homeless and hungry. It includes that inner consecration to Christ, in union with his passion, whereby his holiness is wrought out in us. It includes the constant prayer of Christians everywhere, prayer in which they humble themselves, praying *fiat voluntas*. All this, in depth and breadth, is what the movement to unity must be; and therefore the word "unity" does not suffice to describe it. "I believe in one church"—we did not learn to say that. We learn to say, "I believe in one holy, catholic, and apostolic church," and the notes of the church are a symphony in depth telling of the depth of Christ's prayer and of the depth of its fulfillment.

X

THE KINGDOM OF GOD

Bishop Ramsey was always concerned with political affairs and social policy. As a bishop and later as archbishop he was a member of the House of Lords in the British Parliament, and he spoke there frequently on national policy issues. As Archbishop of Canterbury he was also called upon to give addresses of national importance on social issues. Some of those addresses are included in this section.

His deep interest in such matters was shaped by his life-long commitment to the Christian social teaching that developed in the Church of England from the Catholic Revival of the Oxford Movement and the incarnational theology of F. D. Maurice and his successors. In the address that he gave to the Jubilee Group (an organization in the Church of England which is concerned with the development of Christian social policy) he brought together some of the theological themes which had always affected his thinking, especially the social consequences of belief in the incarnation. He also addressed the issue of Marxism, which, in 1977, dominated much political discussion in Britain and Europe.

As great as his interest was in such matters and as important as his influence was, however, he always returned to the centrality of prayer and worship for the Christian life. He believed that only through our movement to God could we also move toward the world, in order to speak God's name, as he puts it in *Be Still and Know*, "from the middle of the world's darkness and frustration." No better final commentary on Michael Ramsey as a theologian, archbishop, scholar, priest, and friend can be found than this quotation from his last book: "To be near to the love of God is to be near, as Jesus showed, to the darkness of the world. That is the 'place of prayer.'"

∿ 44 ∾

The Catholic Social Tradition Today

From an address given to a conference of the Jubilee Group on 30 June 1977, celebrating the founding of the Guild of St. Matthew by Stewart Headlam.[1]

When it is said that we need to have a "return of the kingdom of God" as the dominant theological idea for Christian social teaching, my response is both No and Yes. There can be a way of using the concept of the kingdom of God which is inadequate and misleading. I think of that aspect which sees it as a kind of commonwealth which can be pictured as an ideal to work for, as embodying the divine will and purpose in history. Now if the divine will is discovered and followed, there will certainly be a society of a better shape, in conformity with God's will. But to be depicting a kind of commonwealth of human affairs towards which we are working can be misleading, for two reasons. Such is the corruption of humanity, and the human ability to corrupt good things, and such is the relativity of the human grasp of God's purpose in different historical situations, that the realization of a divine commonwealth in the world may be something that has still a great number of ups and downs, achievements, corruptions, warnings of divine judgment, and so on. This is one difficulty of thinking of the kingdom of God as a kind of commonwealth.

The second difficulty is this. I think it is very hard to define how far the goal of God's purpose for the world is going to be within

1. Published in Kenneth Leech, *The Gospel, the Catholic Church and the World: The Social Theology of Michael Ramsey* (London: The Jubilee Group, 1990), pp. 21-24.

history or beyond it. If we speak of it in one way, we are caught into speaking of it in the other way. But while I am a little suspicious of a "commonwealth" interpretation of the kingdom of God, and while I believe that its coming into Catholic sociology was in part not derived from Catholic truth but from a kind of liberal Protestant hangover, yet there is a way, theologically, in which the concept of the kingdom of God is vital, and its recovery urgently necessary. The divine sovereignty, and the bringing of human affairs into line with what is known of the divine sovereignty: that enables us to have a bit of a picture of what things will be like when the divine sovereignty is followed, while avoiding any blueprint of it. And we may speak of the divine sovereignty in terms of the reflection of some of God's own attributes in human life: God's compassion perfectly imitated by human creatures in their dealing with one another, and God's justice reproduced in human creatures in imitation of the justice of God. So let the concept of the kingdom of God be a dominant concept, but I believe that certain distinctions are really important.

Secondly, the concept of incarnation. Here not only does Catholic theology give to Catholic social teaching its backbone, but also social teaching may be a means of helping theology not to make such an ass of itself, as it often does, in connection with the incarnation. The depth of Catholic understanding of incarnation has so dropped out of certain theological circles that it appears to be thought that all that is required is a Christ who performs the functions of revealing the will and purpose of God, and who assists the human race in carrying out that will and purpose. There is a world of difference between that, and the incarnation of God whereby humanity through Christ is actually united to God himself, so that incorporation into Christ becomes the way of incorporation into God. That is what incarnation is about: the actual union of humanity with God. When theology gets in a mess about incarnation, it does so through thinking of the incarnation one-sidedly, as God coming down to participate in human affairs, and neglecting the converse truth that humanity is caught up into the life of God through Christ who is born and lives and also ascends. I note with great gratitude that a phrase in the Athanasian Creed is now coming back into Catholic social teaching, and when it comes back into

Christian theology generally we shall be in a better case: "One, not by the conversion of the Godhead into flesh, but by taking of the manhood into God." We can think of the way in which the incarnation not only gives to theology its true shape, but also gives to Christian social teaching both theological backbone and a great deal of practical understanding. Looking at the witness of Stewart Headlam, I would say that much of it is due to the fact that he saw the incarnation as "the taking of manhood into God."

As regards the theological background of Christian social teaching, there is also the doctrine of creation, and the character of the created order as ordained by God. I will not use the term "natural law" since that involves some difficult theological questions of definition. Let me say rather those God-created institutions in the created world such as the state and the family.

We do need to think out again what we mean by the role of the state and the family as God-given institutions. Concerning the state, I think we would apply what we say about the state to the role of smaller-state institutions within it—for example, civic government, county councils, and so on. But should we also apply some of the biblical doctrine of the state to entities which are larger than the state—for example, the European Community, if it emerges and shapes itself? Will our doctrine of the state be applicable to these other institutions? We need to think more then about the organs of sovereignty in the world.

Concerning the family, there are many difficult questions. We are apt to say that monogamous marriage is a part of God's natural law. But this raises difficult questions about, for example, polygamous cultures which have existed for a very long time. We ought to know what to say about them in our doctrines of divine institutions. In the same context, we need to look at human sexuality in the context of the created order. Hitherto the Christian view of sex has seen sex only as part of monogamous marriage. But is this really true? If it does exist apart from monogamous marriage, what do we say about that? These seem to me to be very important questions about the divine order of creation which must form part of the essential background to Christian social teaching....

The question of profit motive. Obviously profit motive is a great evil. It corrupts human lives and it produces in people's way of life something which is utterly contrary to the Creator's purpose. One sure way of making the profit motive impossible is to abolish profit, to create a society in which there is no such thing. But a socialist society which abolishes the profit motive has to go very far indeed in its range. The kind of semi-socialism which we have in Britain, where some things are nationalized and others are not, does not proportionally reduce the profit motive in the least....But if the profit motive is to disappear, the only thing which can make it disappear is the total abolition of profit. That means a Marxist society. Is it possible to combine a Marxist economy with a Christian doctrine of persons in relation to God?

Marxism believes that an inexorable movement is working itself out by which a classless society will come about. A purely economic messianism replaces the Christian messianism. It seems to me conceivable that the Marxists may be right, that there will inevitably be a classless society. If so, I want to say Yes. But what I refuse to do is to identify that with the kingdom of God, or to agree that it will necessarily be better, unless human beings know who they are—God's children and creatures. The emerging classless society may turn out to be pretty horrible unless meanwhile people are converted to their true relationship with God. So Marxism may be true as economic fact, but false as an adequate statement of the human person in relation to the universe.

∾   45   ∾

The Death Penalty

A speech given to the House of Lords in 1965;
from *Canterbury Pilgrim*, pp. 139-140.

I believe that retribution is a necessary and valid aspect of punishment. I should wish to emphasize that retribution need not imply vindictiveness or hatred or vengeance. It does mean that wrongdoers suffer punishment because they deserve to; and the recognition on their part that they are getting something they deserve is a necessary step towards their reformation. And if the crime has been a terrible one, the penalty will be a terrible one.

But in trying to set out what I believe to be Christian principles in this matter, I go at once to two other considerations. First there ought to be beyond the penalty the possibility of reclamation. I mean the possibility of the person being alive, repentant, and different. If this can happen in this world, and not only for the world to come, we should strive for that to be so. Secondly, there ought to be recognition of the fact that the taking of life as a penalty does devalue human life. It means society saying, in effect: "This man has killed someone. Very well; we will kill him too." This does not enhance the sacredness of human life. I believe that it devalues it further.

I am very conscious that these considerations have to be weighed against the other consideration which has been so prominent in the discussion—namely, the need for deterrence. Terrible crime needs to be deterred. Victims must be protected, and all of us feel to the uttermost for victims and their families. If there were convincing evidence that any penalty is a unique deterrent, then I should feel obliged to let that weigh very heavily in the scale against those basic considerations which I have tried to set out.

Now it is asked: if not the death penalty, then what? I take up my own phrase, "a terrible punishment for a terrible crime." Here the arguments seem to me to be very strong for the life sentence rather than a judicial sentence for a certain term of years. There is the argument that the judge cannot know at the outset what someone is going to be like after nine, ten, eleven, or twelve years, or how the person should be best treated, both for public safety and for his or her own good, after that time. That consideration is a strong one, and it concerns both security and the protection of the people, as well as what is good in the reclamation of the criminal.

But I would add this consideration, too, in connection with the life sentence. The sentence for the crime of murder ought, I believe, to have what I call a retributive moral seriousness about it: therefore, I believe that the life sentence is right, even though it again and again, and perhaps almost always, be mitigated in practice. The life sentence says, in effect, to a convicted murderer:

"You have outraged society by killing one of your fellows. You must expect no claim to your old place in society for a very long time, not, indeed, until society can be told that you are on the way to being a different sort of person from what you are now." I believe that, thus understood, a life sentence carries with it a moral meaning.

⤳ **46** ⤳

Abortion

An address to the Convocation of Canterbury on 17 January 1967, in reference to the report *Abortion—An Ethical Discussion*, passed by the Church Assembly the previous year; from *Canterbury Pilgrim*, pp. 163-167.

The emphasis upon this phrase ["the sanctity of life for the fetus"] goes back to the report. I quote one of its key passages:

> If we are to remain faithful to the tradition, we have to assert, as normative, the general inviolability of the fetus; to defend, as a first principle, its right to live and develop; and then to lay the burden of proof to the contrary firmly on those who, in particular cases, would wish to extinguish that right on the ground that it was in conflict with another or others with a higher claim to recognition. Only so, in fact, can we maintain the *intention* of the moral tradition, which is to uphold the value and importance of human life. For invariably in this discussion the question must arise, which life? (pp. 31-32)

It is well that we should now remind ourselves of this statement of first principles because in the debates occasioned by two successive bills dealing with the matter in the past year first principles have become somewhat obscured by the sheer mass of detailed discussion of how much or how little.

We know that some people desire legal facilities for abortion going far beyond any of the current proposals and would like to make abortion lawful virtually at will. If we remember that this is to revert to the state of things in the ancient world before Christianity it helps us to see what the role of Christianity has been in this matter....

When it brought its vastly enhanced view of the sanctity of human life, Christianity condemned both abortion and infanticide, which had been widespread in the ancient world. In condemning both abortion and infanticide the church from the time of Constantine virtually equated the two. Both were the destruction of life, both were murder. Though there was no invariable doctrine as to the point in time in which human existence with a soul was held to begin, yet the destruction of the fetus was the destruction of a life sacred to God and to humanity. From this there followed the absolutist principle in refusing any and every abortion as unlawful....

It is indeed very hard to be certain how many days or weeks after conception the fetus is to be identified with a human personality. It is uncertain at what stage terms like "person" or "human being" should be used. It is thus misleading to identify abortion and infanticide: both devalue human life, but they are not identical and it is wrong to stir emotion by identifying them. Yet the authors of the Report continue, and I believe that we shall be right to continue, to see as one of Christianity's great gifts to the world the belief that the human fetus is to be reverenced as the embryo of a life capable of coming to reflect the glory of God whatever trials it may be going to face.

But does this mean the absolutist position against abortion? No, the absolutist position is strained to absurdity when it is seen that it can in certain circumstances condemn both the mother and the fetus to death, and thereby pose the question: Should not the one *or* the other be saved if possible? This leads on to the view that the underlying principle, rather than the letter, of the older Christian tradition demands that there may be the choice between the life and mental and bodily health of the mother and the life of the fetus. There are occasions when the latter, which is an embryonic and potential life, may be sacrificed for the former, which is a life already....

In drawing the line where I have suggested that it should be drawn, what are the decisive considerations? There is the consideration of compassion. But to this must be added the consideration of justice, as we try to weigh one set of rights against another, and one set of risks against another. And besides both compassion and justice there are the two Christian convictions of which we must never lose sight. The first is that the eternal destiny with God in heaven, possible to every child conceived in the mother's womb, matters supremely. The second is that while we must strive to remove suffering we do not foreclose the ways in which in the midst of frustrations and handicaps some of the glories of human lives may be seen.

⌁   47   ∿

The Family

An address given in 1972; from *Canterbury Pilgrim*, pp. 168-170.

We who are Christians believe that the family is part of God's scheme of things. When men and women take part in the procreation of children they have the wonderful privilege of sharing in God's creation of human life, and they are called to do this in God's way. And God's way means that procreation takes place not anyhow but by a man and woman who are joined together in a lifelong union, a union in which they give themselves to one another until death parts them. This is the atmosphere of love and stability into which, in God's design, children are born. And having been born in a family they are loved, cared for, and protected, and they grow up in the freedom and discipline of mutual love and care for one another. So when children go out to take their part in the world their role in their own family is not left behind but lasts as a permanent part of their lives. The happiest families are not introverted and wrapped up in their own circle but outgoing as a part of the wider community.

The family today faces a scene of immense social change, and it often has to express its own unchanging character amid conditions different from those of the past. One big change is that far more women are going out to work, and the roles of the man and the woman in the home may not be distinguished in all the same ways as in the past: both may be sharing in the washing-up and both may be sharing in the earning of the family income. And there may be long distances between home and work. Such is the setting in which the family virtues have to be rediscovered and practiced.

Then there is the frequent conflict of generations. More than in the past, the young are striking out into intellectual independence and revolt against tradition. The need is to help the young to discover that Christian morality is not a negative tradition of rules and prohibitions but an adventure of freedom in the unselfish service of God and neighbor.

So these immense changes of social scene bring strains on the family. And sometimes there is the further strain of very unsuitable housing, or the difficulty of getting any housing at all. If we care about the family, this should be high among our priorities of concern.

Then there are the strains due to what is called the sexual revolution. I hope we welcome the greater openness about sex, as I am sure the old puritanical idea that sex should always be hushed up was unwholesome and did harm. We must avoid a kind of backlash towards puritanism. But sex is the bond of a union between two persons in their totality as persons; that is its true meaning. And today we have to witness against all those influences which separate sex from human personality and treat it as an excitement on a sub-human plane. The commercial exploitation of sex is horrible, yes horrible.

Then there is the idea which some are proclaiming that the family is an outmoded institution and should be superseded by some other pattern of human relationships. I am sure we cannot meet this propaganda effectively by denunciations. Rather must we show that the family has its own unique role within a society based on justice, fellowship, and the true freedom found in the service of God. Our concern for the family goes hand-in-hand with our concern for justice in the community of which family is a part.

Above all there is the need for the most thorough education in the meaning of the family, and education from the earliest years. Christians will cherish an education about the family which is rooted in the truth about the family in God's design and purpose, an education in which human relationships are linked with the knowledge and service of God. But when people are not Christians, then what? There the need is for the best possible teaching based upon the natural law of morality....To do so does not belittle the paramount importance of specific Christian teaching where it can be given and received.

Far more must be done to help those who are getting married to realize what is meant by the covenant to a lifelong union, and to be ready for the problems of parenthood....

The forces which threaten the family are deep and widespread in our society, forces social and economic as well as moral. If we are wise we shall not concentrate on denunciations of evil in the sexual sphere but shall try to cope at every point with the sickness in society which leads to such evil. For us who are Christians there is no substitute for bringing men and women and children to the knowledge and love of God, and it is this which gives to the family its deepest meaning and strength.

◡ **48** ◡

Nonviolence

An address given at a commemoration of Gandhi in St. Paul's Cathedral in 1969; from *Canterbury Pilgrim*, pp. 137-138.

We who are Christians proclaim that Christ is the perfect and final revelation of God, "God of God, light of light," as we say in our creed. At the same time we reverence the divine image in every person, and we believe that the divine light has shone in good people of other religions and wherever that light shines we know we are on sacred ground. It was in that spirit that I as a Christian went barefoot to the tomb of Gandhi when I was in India seven years ago....

How providential it was to have such a man at such a time. The vast population of India with its religious fervor, its coming into control of its own destiny, its deep divisions, its terrible poverty, in its midst had a leader who every day of his life made nonviolence his ideal, put simplicity of life before wealth and comfort, put the things of the spirit before material things, made the cause of the poor and outcast his own, and sealed it all by a martyr's death. What a gift he was to India!

It was not to India alone that Gandhi was a gift, and is today a lesson and a challenge. We talk about spiritual values, but material things easily fill our minds and our activities. How Gandhi shows us the happiness of the way of simplicity. We have a world where violence seems to increase, and the meeting of violence by violence seems the order of the day. How Gandhi shows what nonviolence can achieve. We have a world where the voice of conscience, the voice of moral authority is mixed with so many voices of compromise and expediency, and doing right for the sake of doing right is often far to seek. How Gandhi shows us the rule of conscience in human affairs. On the mount in Galilee Christ said: "Blessed are the poor in spirit"; "Blessed are the peacemakers"; "Blessed are those who hunger and thirst after righteousness." It was that part of Christ's teaching which appealed to Gandhi. It was that part of Christ's teaching which he followed.

The light shone, and the darkness did not overcome it. We greet today the peoples of India, praying that they may have the peace, the unity, the justice for which Gandhi worked and died. And we pray for ourselves that to us this same light will shine and we shall follow it.

⨯ **49** ⨯

Christianity and Violence

A lecture given in Cambridge in 1972;
from *Canterbury Pilgrim*, pp. 129-136.

Through the centuries probably only a minority of considering Christians have held that Christ's teaching demands the totally pacifist position. I would hold myself that the injunction to turn the other cheek and to offer no resistance to evil, like many other of Christ's injunctions, concerns motive. Faced with a violent attack the follower of Christ must have total selflessness in motive; so far as his or her own pride or comfort or security is concerned, the Christian must be ready to accept death and have no self-concern. But given that selflessness of motive which Christ demands, the Christian may strike, or risk killing, or even kill if the concern is to protect others, whether family, friends, neighbors, enemies, or the community itself. It has been found possible, however hazardous, to strike in defense of others without hatred, anger, or self-concern; and conversely it is possible to be physically passive while bearing anger and hatred. It is such considerations which cause many conscientious Christians not to endorse total pacifism. So too there is Christ's recognition of the state as the organ of order and justice, a recognition which St. Paul and St. Peter enhanced and developed.

Perhaps a stronger argument for total pacifism is the centrality of the cross in Christianity with its corollary of the identity of divine sovereignty and sacrificial love. Is it not by the total acceptance of the principle of the cross that evil in the world is to be overcome? Even here, however, we note that the principle of self-sacrifice can have a variety of manifestations in different contexts, and that in Christ's teaching the doctrine of the divine judgment upon the world's wrongdoing includes the working out of calamity and pain in the disciplines of humility into God's obedience....

It is with [the just war theory informing its thinking] that western Christendom has passed through the centuries and entered the modern world. Now I ask what is happening in the modern world to these traditional concepts.

First, the older doctrine of the just war has become difficult to uphold with conviction—not impossible in any context, perhaps, but difficult. We may still think of possible limited wars to which criteria of justice might be applied; but Vietnam with its continuing destruction without winners is no convincing illustration. When, however, the weapons of war are such that a possible result of a war is the indiscriminate destruction of nations on either side and perhaps the doom of all civilization, how do the old criteria apply? It is partly this consideration which has given a big impetus to total pacifism in recent times. More Christians are convinced pacifists than used to be the case. And the increase of what may be called "near pacifism" is greater still.

Second, there has been within movements for social change or revolution a rise of the ideology of nonviolence. Perhaps this is the reflection within states and countries of the pacifist trend about relations between states and countries. Gandhi in India, Chief Luthuli in South Africa, and Martin Luther King in America have all been instances of this. I think that a range of different ideas has been at work among these movements and their leaders: at one end the religious idea that to witness and to suffer patiently is itself a spiritual power by which evil is overcome, and at the other end ideas more akin to a general strike or a mass protest, where the right course is to upset the community by weight of numbers while avoiding any killing or causing pain. In neither case have we seen the end of these ideas or their application, whether martyrdom in the spirit of the cross of Christ or protest in the spirit of a general strike.

Third, while in both these ways the nonviolent attitudes have grown considerably, there has also been the upsurging of new demands for violent revolution as both a good idea to hold and a good thing to do. Nothing accelerated this more than the story of [Nelson] Mandela and his friends in South Africa. Long, patient use of nonviolent methods failed, and they were crushed by the regime's own use of violence. So they asked: "What then is left to us but violence?" The situation fitted pretty closely to St. Thomas Aquinas's classic words about the just war: "the violent overthrow of [a tyrannical] regime does not partake of the nature of sedition." But inevitably there is the anxiety lest rebellion in desperate circumstances may issue in enhanced suffering for the very people it is designed to help....

So we have seen in relation to the world scene an increasing pacifist trend within Christian thought, overtaken by a revival of the doctrine of violence in relation to particular situations. It is in this scene that we have to make our own decisions as Christians about right and wrong. There are probably many of us who in worldly terms veer towards pacifism, as there can be no just holocaust; and then feel the case for just rebellions in more limited contexts. What are we to think or do?

I suggest first that we must avoid positions which are so inconsistent as to involve a kind of Pharisaism. We cannot applaud Europeans who resisted the tyranny of a Hitler and then be shocked when Africans want to resist a tyrannical regime today; we can discuss the wisdom or the expediency, but we cannot indulge in facile moral censures. We too easily form a habit of exculpating the violence in our own sphere of history and censuring the violence of other races.

Then, we need to avoid a selective mentality in our moral judgments generally. There are reasons for our concern about white racism through our own involvement in it. But we need to remember that there are African countries where tribal majorities are unjust to tribal minorities, and where killing and suffering have had appalling dimensions. We need to remember the sufferings, which still continue, of Christians and Jews and others under communist regimes in eastern Europe. Neither the right eye nor the left eye alone can easily see the whole field of human suffering and moral judgment....

Then we cannot honorably commend to other people idealistic Christian actions which we ourselves are unwilling to practice or share. This error can take two forms. We can encourage people to belligerence while we keep out of the conflict, or we can say to other people that of course their Christian calling is to suffer patiently in the spirit of the cross of Christ. In either case we can safely say anything at all only if we are ready to be one with those who are suffering. It is this that is imperative; it is also this that is sometimes so hard as to be near-impossible. That is our tragic situation.

So I put to you these guidelines. They do not answer our questions, but at least they can sheer us away from those ethical absurdities which make a right judgment impossible....

Hope lies in the existence of Christians who know that these questions about violence and nonviolence are crucial for humanity, who do not claim to know all the answers but are passionately keen to try to find answers which are both intellectually serious and congruous with the Spirit of Christ. I have done no more than suggest to you some of the pitfalls of inconsistency to be avoided and some of the paths to be followed. I believe that if we follow these paths we may often discover in particular situations what the Spirit of Christ who is the Spirit of truth will show us if we ask in integrity of mind and sincerity of prayer. Some differences of view may never be resolved, or not resolved for a long time. If my own view is, as it is, not the view of total pacifism, I shrink from commending it to you as the one Christian view, as I remember that two of the best Christians I ever knew personally differed about this. William Temple was, very gently, a nonpacifist. Charles Raven was, violently, a pacifist. In either case we are called upon to be without concern for our own selves, to be ready to identify ourselves with those who suffer, to be undiscriminating in our distributing of moral censures, and to be sure that our striving for justice and humanity will have fulfillment in a world beyond this. To emphasize the otherworldly goal of Christianity is no escapism, no slackening of our hope for God's reign here in this world. Rather does it give us the true perspective of our present conflicts, showing us that many of our judgments can only be relative, that we never know as much as we think we know, and that every man, woman, and child created by God is eternally in God's keeping, as we look to a day when we shall love as we are loved and know as we are known.

✥ **50** ✥

To Pray is to Serve

An address given at the consecration of the new chapel at St. Mary's Abbey, West Malling, 20 June 1966; from *Canterbury Pilgrim*, pp. 65-68.

Within the family of Christ's people there are many diverse vocations. Many, indeed the majority, of Christians are called by God to marriage, the family, and the home. Through the centuries, Christ has called some to the religious life in the threefold vows of poverty, chastity, obedience. Here is an intensely evangelical part of Christianity, rooted in the gospel story. Jesus calls some to literal poverty. Jesus spoke of the call to celibacy as given to those able to receive it. And while all Christians must obey, Christ's call to poverty and to chastity has with it necessarily a very distinctive obedience.

And as to the religious vows. These are not presumptuous. These are not a piece of Pelagian self-determination. Rather, the vows of religion mean the total acceptance of the call of God and the gift from God—an acceptance "by faith alone" and "by grace alone." To God alone be the glory.

Now there was perhaps never a time when the religious life was more significant in Christendom and in the world than today. If God calls and if God disposes gifts, the call and the gifts are true and valid in their own right because they are God's; yet we are able to see how God's call and God's gifts can answer the problems and needs of different epochs in history. Today there is the love of pleasure, self-pleasing, willfulness, the belief that life is best with no authority at all, and it is against that that the call to obedience in the religious life is so very significant as a witness to the truth of God. Today the love of money, and the spirit of getting and grabbing is widespread, and against that the joy of poverty in Christian vocation is so very significant. And today, too, lust and self-expression, and self-expression as an unthinking ideal, are widespread, and against that the call to the beauty and joy of chastity is very significant also.

And as to the life of a religious community. Here its stability and its permanence has a telling, divine meaning. Human life flits, these days, from one excitement to another, from one novelty to another, a little of this and a little of that, and the bondage to the passing moment is widespread. And hence a witness to God is borne by the stability of a Christian home and a Christian marriage, "those whom God has joined together, let no man put asunder," a union of lives "until death us do part." So, too, a witness to God is borne by the stability of a religious community. It stands for the permanence of the vocation in its members, but it stands also for a witness to things that are not shaken, to truths and ideals which are not of any one age but reach across the centuries, a ladder set up and its top reaches to heaven (Gen. 28:12)....

Now the Benedictine way is a way of worship and work; *laborare est orare, orare est laborare.* As such, the Benedictine way is an epitome of Christian life itself. Now, ideally, work and worship are utterly one. Every deed of service of the Christian hand or the Christian brain is a lifting up of the soul to God, and the top of the ladder reaches to heaven. Equally, every lifting up of the soul to God in adoration is a profound service of the human race, and the ladder is indeed set upon this earth. But in our present inevitable imperfection our lives have to be divided, divided into those times which we call "saying our prayers," and the times which we call "getting on with our work." And this dichotomy, present in all Christians in the world, appears no less in the religious life; and hence in the history of the religious life there are communities which use the phrase "the mixed life." For them prayer, worship, is the supreme priority; the Liturgy and the Office and personal prayer come always first, and first unshakably. But besides the prayer a community may be dedicated to particular works in education or evangelism, or the care of the sick or the poor, or many kinds of service to humanity and to human crafts.

Here at West Malling is an abbey where the work is not prayer plus this, plus that, and plus the other, but where the work is prayer, plus prayer, plus prayer, plus prayer. The prayer is itself the work, and the service of the world is itself the prayer offered to the most high God on the world's behalf. And this means an apartness, an apartness like the apartness of our Lord in the Judean desert: praying and fighting on behalf of us all, on behalf of the human race. It is an apartness, a being with God, but also on behalf of the human race with its sins, its joys, and its sorrows.

The apartness, as all Christian apartness, must be real and costly. The nearness must be real and costly too. So it is that wherever there is a community, a family of Christian people dedicated supremely to prayer on behalf of the world and to prayer on behalf of all of us—the sinful, struggling members of the Christian church in our various offices and callings—we know that in that community and in that family there is care and help and love and we are understood and prayed for and cared for and helped very mightily. And so it is that many individual men and women and children in the church and beyond the church know that here, as in many another house devoted to prayer, their sins and their troubles are cared for and they are being greatly helped. Similarly many distresses in the church, in this country, and in the wider world are being likewise helped and served. The door of prayer towards heaven, towards the heart of God, is always a door of love into the world of human needs....

But the ladder of Christian prayer not only reaches to heaven and rests most firmly on earth. More than that, it unites heaven and earth very closely, because the ladder is Jesus, the Incarnate Lord. In him, through him, we share today in the prayers and praises of the blessed saints in heaven. In him, through him, we touch with our prayers the sins and sorrows of humankind. And in him, through him, our prayers shall be made one in him, as he is in the Father in the bond of the Holy Ghost. To whom be glory, praise, and thanksgiving from angels and from all people, now and for evermore.

ᔔ   **51**   ᔓ

Christian Spirituality and the Modern World

A lecture to the *Cercle Oecumenique* in the University of Louvain,
3 May 1963; from *Canterbury Essays and Addresses*, pp. 26-30.

It is clear that with the involvement of service to the world there is united, in true Christian spirituality, a spirit of detachment. While Christian people strive to heal the world's ills by their service and charity, it is for them also to point to the ill which is at the root of all ills, the estrangement of the world from God, and to witness to the reality of God himself. They do so by the depth of their communion with him and by their humility before him. The unknown writer of the Epistle to Diognetus said, "As the soul is in the body so are the Christians in the world." The Christians serve a world which has lost its soul by the lifting up of their own souls in adoration.

Adoration and communion with God is, however, always the soul's response to God's own gift. This divine gift is seen in the Bible as the Word of God. The Word of God is both speech and action. By the Word of God the people of Israel were delivered from bondage in Egypt and made the recipients of the divine covenant and the divine law at Sinai. So too by the Word of God the people of the new Israel were delivered from sin and death and given the new covenant in the blood of Jesus the Messiah. The action of the Divine Word, both in the Old Testament and in the New, creates and sustains a people, the church, the family of the redeemed; and it is within this corporate life that the divine gifts are brought to individual souls. The sacred scriptures tell of the divine history and the divine gifts, and in the *lectio divina* the members of the church refresh their souls with the knowledge of them and are drawn to the response of thanksgiving and adoration.

But there is more. The Word of God was made flesh in the birth of Jesus, and came to indwell the church through the sacraments, and the action of the Holy Spirit. The divine gift is thus not only the record of God's gracious acts long ago in the days of the Bible. It is also the very presence of Jesus, God and Man, here and now—contemporary: Jesus who is *Verbum caro factum* and is no less *Christus crucifixus resurrectus et glorificatus.* The mystery of the church is *Christus in vobis, spes gloriae.*

In the worship of the church there are three chief elements: the eucharistic liturgy, the divine office, and personal prayer, both vocal and mental. The last may happen in groups and families as well as individually. I use the terms—liturgy, divine office, personal prayer—familiar to you and familiar also to me as an Anglican. In each of the three elements—eucharist, office, personal prayer—there is the divine gift and the human response.

The eucharist is the center and norm of all worship. There the Divine Word is revealed in the lections and propers for the nourishment of our souls. But at the climax of the rite, through the consecration prayer, the whole mystery of Christ as priest, victim, and victor, is present. In the eucharistic canon gift and response find fullness of expression, and both are inseparable from Christ himself. The divine gift to us is Christ, and so too the response from human beings is Christ, himself our sacrifice. Our own response is made only as we are ourselves "in Christ." In the words of an Anglican eucharistic hymn, we say:

> Look, Father, look on his anointed face,
> And only look on us as found in him.

But let me quote also the words of St. Augustine:

> This is the sacrifice of Christians, the many one body in Christ, which also the church celebrates in the sacrament of the altar, familiar to the faithful, where it is shown to be that in this thing which she offers she herself is offered.[2]

I speak of liturgy as a fact in Christendom which has appeared in a variety of forms and phases, with different spiritual emphases. In the Latin rite there is a vivid sense of the cross where sinful people look upon him whom their sins have pierced and know that

---

2. *The City of God,* 10.6.

in Jesus crucified alone is salvation, though the thought of the heavenly tabernacle is never far away. In the liturgies of the Orthodox East, both Greek and Slavonic, the joy of the resurrection is prominent and the worshipers know themselves to be already in the heavenly places in Christ. In the case of Anglican liturgy it is necessary for a right understanding to see not only the rite in England, but also the rites in the United States (derived from Scotland), in Canada, in the West Indies, in India, and in various parts of Africa, giving as they do a picture of a growing liturgical life mindful alike of the one sacrifice of Calvary and of the heavenly priesthood of our Lord. Today liturgical movements in many parts of Christendom put a renewed emphasis upon the participation of the faithful in the liturgy and upon the down-to-earth aspect of the liturgy as the means of consecrating the common, everyday life of the people to God. In this way liturgy is seen to belong alike to the involvement and to the detachment in the mission of the church.

While, however, the liturgy is the norm of worship, there is the need for the divine gift so to penetrate the souls of Christian people that they are drawn into the deep response of penitence, love, and adoration, through meditative and contemplative prayer. Without meditative and contemplative prayer the sacramental life can become shallow and formal and can lack interior depth. It is essential that the liturgical movement with its great emphasis upon the corporate action of the faithful in worship be accompanied by no less emphasis upon interior prayer.

It would be rash of me to venture far into the controversial subject of the relation between meditation and contemplation, and between activity and passivity in prayer. But these matters are fundamental. In modern times in our Anglican Church as well as in Catholic spirituality in Europe there came about a tendency to regard discursive meditation (called by whatever name) as a norm for most Christians and to think of any approach to contemplative prayer as a thing far removed and characteristic of advanced souls or mystics. But we have seen the recovery of an older tradition of spirituality, whereby elementary contemplation has a place not only for advanced souls but for ordinary Christians too. This older tradition is beautifully described by Dom Cuthbert Butler, a former abbot of the Benedictine monastery of Downside, in his book

Western Mysticism. I would myself humbly dare to say that whereas discursive meditation can become all too easily a cerebral process, putting too much strain upon the powers of the mind, affective prayer or elementary contemplation is God's gift to many who are ready to reach out to God in desire and longing. This contemplative prayer is something which God can grant to souls who reach out to him in their poverty, their want, their childlike desire. It is a prayer which some writers describe as coming "from the ground of the soul." I believe that the capacity of the ordinary Christian for contemplation is greater by far than some of our theories of the spiritual life have allowed.

It is in the measure in which the contemplative spirit is present in the church that the reality of God will be grasped within the church's multiple activities. [The contemplative spirit] demands a will for leisure and passivity in the midst of ceaseless activity. I recall the words of Fénelon in a letter to a French duke of the time, "I want to help you to find how to lead a very full and yet a leisurely life." That is a prime requisite for Christian spirituality in the modern world.

∿ **52** ∿

The Place of Prayer

From *Be Still and Know*, pp. 11-14.

There are many people who warm to the Christian faith and yet find the idea of prayer perplexing or even intellectually suspect. It is sometimes asked: amid the vast range of desperate human need can we believe that a God of love and compassion gives selective favors to certain people because some other people may have prayed for them? Others ask: are we sure that the praying which goes on in churches and elsewhere really affects the course of events in the world around us?

We need, however, to see Christian prayer not as an isolated religious exercise but as an aspect of a many-sided converse between human beings and their Creator. In the Christian belief God makes himself known to humankind in many ways: through the beauty of nature, through the stirrings of conscience, through inspired individuals and writings, through events of history, and supremely through Jesus Christ. To these "utterances" of God the human response is no less multiple: by gratitude and trust and love, by awe and wonder, by grief and contrition, by acts of practical service and the pursuit of a way of life. In this response there is movement of the heart and mind and will towards God, partly but not always wholly expressed in words. The entire God-human relationship is often described by the biblical writers, Jewish and Christian, in the images of speaking and hearing. But verbal conversation, as when a voice says "Samuel, Samuel" and a response comes "Here I am," is but a small fraction in a relationship containing word and silence, passivity and action. Such is the context of prayer in Christianity.

It seems to follow that, in understanding the true nature of prayer, it is a mistake to draw too rigidly the frontier between prayer and life. The separation of them, which has sadly recurred in history, can lead to caricatures of both. Thus prayer can become a pious or aesthetic or cultural pursuit, whose goal seems less than the God who loves humankind; and the Christian life can become a kind of aggressive busyness which misses the humility and the inner peace which communion with God can bring.

If the interweaving of prayer and life within the converse with God is realized, then the two questions mentioned at the beginning of this prologue may appear less daunting.

First: Does petitionary prayer imply an arbitrary selectivity in God's graciousness? It need not do so. If God is a God of love and compassion who uses the cooperation of human wills to fulfill his purpose, the petitionary prayer of a Christian will be both an offering of oneself and a caring request on behalf of others, both a "Lord, make me an instrument of your peace" and a "Lord, use my caring to bless X and Y and Z." When people thus put their caring at God's disposal they will be confident that good will come to X and Y and Z, but they will not suppose that God's graciousness will halt with them. The teaching of Jesus suggests that God wants us to bring our specific desires to him, and to try to relate them to his purpose. We need not think that God will limit his use of our caring to those whom we name because we care.

Second: Is it credible that the praying which goes on in churches and elsewhere makes a difference to the world, apart perhaps from those who do the praying? If prayer and life are interwoven in the way described, then the right question may be not, "What good does prayer do?" but, "What good does the praying Christian do?" The praying Christian is one whose prayer is part of a converse with God which includes actions and orientations as well as words. Through the centuries, despite the failures and the scandals, the impact of Christianity in creating not a few Christ-like lives has been through Christians for whom prayer has been an integral part of their sharing in the divine love. The promises of Jesus about the results of prayer are corroborated by recurring empirical evidence.

At the present time there has been in the West a trend of feeling towards the contemplative aspect of prayer, and many have looked to Eastern religions for contemplative practice, partly as a result of the church's sad neglect of its own contemplative tradition. It is not, however, always realized either by seekers of contemplation or by its critics that contemplation is not only a quest of the inner peace of God but an exposure to the love of God with intercessory outreach. We learn from a contemplative such as Thomas Merton that the movement of the soul away from the world into the life of God is a movement also into the world's heart. The renewal of contemplation in the church may help to renew caring service towards the world.

Concerning intercession: the church is called to be a community which speaks to the world in God's name and speaks to God from the middle of the world's darkness and frustration. The prayer with beautiful buildings and lovely music must be a prayer which also speaks from the places where men and women work, or lack work, and are sad and hungry, suffer and die. To be near to the love of God is to be near, as Jesus showed, to the darkness of the world. That is the "place of prayer."

Cowley Publications is a ministry of the Society of St. John the Evangelist, a religious community for men in the Episcopal Church. Emerging from the Society's tradition of prayer, theological reflection, and diversity of mission, the press is centered in the rich heritage of the Anglican Communion.

Cowley Publications seeks to provide books, audio cassettes, and other resources for the ongoing theological exploration and spiritual development of the Episcopal Church and others in the body of Christ. To this end, it is dedicated to developing a new generation of theological writers, encouraging them to produce timely, creative, and stimulating publications of excellence, and making these publications available widely, reaching both clergy and lay persons.